Washington Nationals 2021

A Baseball Companion

Edited by Steven Goldman and Bret Sayre

Baseball Prospectus

Craig Brown, Associate Editor
Robert Au, Harry Pavlidis and Amy Pircher, Statistics Editors

Copyright © 2021 by DIY Baseball, LLC.
All rights reserved

This book or any part thereof may not be reproduced or transmitted in any form or by any means, electronic or mechanical, including photocopying, recording, or by any information storage and retrieval system, without permission in writing from the publisher.

Limit of Liability/Disclaimer of Warranty: While the publisher and the author have used their best efforts in preparing this book, they make no representations or warranties with respect to the accuracy or completeness of the contents of this book and specifically disclaim any implied warranties of merchantability or fitness for a particular purpose. No warranty may be created or extended by sales representatives or written sales materials. The advice and strategies contained herein may not be suitable for your situation. You should consult with a professional where appropriate. Neither the publisher nor the author shall be liable for any loss of profit or any other commercial damages, including but not limited to special, incidental, consequential, or other damages.

Library of Congress Cataloging-in-Publication Data:
paperback
ISBN-13: 978-1-950716-83-8

Project Credits
Cover Design: Ginny Searle
Interior Design and Production: Amy Pircher, Robert Au
Layout: Amy Pircher, Robert Au

Baseball icon courtesy of Uberux, from https://www.shareicon.net/author/uberux

Ballpark diagram courtesy of Lou Spirito/THIRTY81 Project, https://thirty81project.com/

Manufactured in the United States of America
10 9 8 7 6 5 4 3 2 1

Table of Contents

Statistical Introduction v

Part 1: Team Analysis

Performance Graphs 3
2020 Team Performance 4
2021 Team Projections 5
Team Personnel 6
Nationals Park Stats 7
Nationals Team Analysis 9

Part 2: Player Analysis

Nationals Player Analysis 16
Nationals Prospects 87

Part 3: Featured Articles

Nationals All-Time Top 10 Players 99
    by Rob Mains

A Taxonomy of 2020 Abnormalities 105
    by Rob Mains

Tranches of WAR 111
    by Russell A. Carleton

Secondhand Sport 117
    by Patrick Dubuque

Steve Dalkowski Dreaming 121
    by Steven Goldman

A Reward For A Functioning Society 125
    by Cory Frontin and Craig Goldstein

Index of Names 129

Statistical Introduction

Sports are, fundamentally, a blend of athletic endeavor and storytelling. Baseball, like any other sport, tells its stories in so many ways: in the arc of a game from the stands or a season from the box scores, in photos, or even in numbers. At Baseball Prospectus, we understand that statistics don't replace observation or any of baseball's stories, but complement everything else that makes the game so much fun.

What stats help us with is with patterns and precision, variance and value. This book can help you learn things you may not see from watching a game or hundred, whether it's the path of a career over time or the breadth of the entire MLB. We'd also never ask you to choose between our numbers and the experience of viewing a game from the cheap seats or the comfort of your home; our publication combines running the numbers with observations and wisdom from some of the brightest minds we can find. But if you *do* want to learn more about the numbers beyond what's on the backs of player jerseys, let us help explain.

Offense

We've revised our methodology for determining batting value. Long-time readers of the book will notice that we've retired True Average in favor of a new metric: Deserved Runs Created Plus (DRC+). Developed by Jonathan Judge and our stats team, this statistic measures everything a player does at the plate–reaching base, hitting for power, making outs, and moving runners over–and puts it on a scale where 100 equals league-average performance. A DRC+ of 150 is terrific, a DRC+ of 100 is average and a DRC+ of 75 means you better be an excellent defender.

DRC+ also does a better job than any of our previous metrics in taking contextual factors into account. The model adjusts for how the park affects performance, but also for things like the talent of the opposing pitcher, value of different types of batted-ball events, league, temperature and other factors. It's able to describe a player's expected offensive contribution than any other statistic we've found over the years, and also does a better job of predicting future performance as well.

The other aspect of run-scoring is baserunning, which we quantify using Baserunning Runs. BRR not only records the value of stolen bases (or getting caught in the act), but also accounts for all the stuff that doesn't show up on the back of a baseball card: a runner's ability to go first to third on a single, or advance on a fly ball.

Defense

Where offensive value is *relatively* easy to identify and understand, defensive value is … not. Over the past dozen years, the sabermetric community has focused mostly on stats based on zone data: a real-live human person records the type of batted ball and estimated landing location, and models are created that give expected outs. From there, you can compare fielders' actual outs to those expected ones. Simple, right?

Unfortunately, zone data has two major issues. First, zone data is recorded by commercial data providers who keep the raw data private unless you pay for it. (All the statistics we build in this book and on our website use public data as inputs.) That hurts our ability to test assumptions or duplicate results. Second, over the years it has become apparent that there's quite a bit of "noise" in zone-based fielding analysis. Sometimes the conclusions drawn from zone data don't hold up to scrutiny, and sometimes the different data provided by different providers don't look anything alike, giving wildly different results. Sometimes the hard-working professional stringers or scorers might unknowingly inflict unconscious bias into the mix: for example good fielders will often be credited with more expected outs despite the data, and ballparks with high press boxes tend to score more line drives than ones with a lower press box.

Enter our Fielding Runs Above Average (FRAA). For most positions, FRAA is built from play-by-play data, which allows us to avoid the subjectivity found in many other fielding metrics. The idea is this: count how many fielding plays are made by a given player and compare that to expected plays for an average fielder at their position (based on pitcher ground ball tendencies and batter handedness). Then we adjust for park and base-out situations.

When it comes to catchers, our methodology is a little different thanks to the laundry list of responsibilities they're tasked with beyond just, well, catching and throwing the ball. By now you've probably heard about "framing" or the art of making umpires more likely to call balls outside the strike zone for strikes. To put this into one tidy number, we incorporate pitch tracking data (for the years it exists) and adjust for important factors like pitcher, umpire, batter and home-field advantage using a mixed-model approach. This grants us a number for how many strikes the catcher is personally adding to (or subtracting from) his pitchers' performance … which we then convert to runs added or lost using linear weights.

Framing is one of the biggest parts of determining catcher value, but we also take into account blocking balls from going past, whether a scorer deems it a passed ball or a wild pitch. We use a similar approach—one that really benefits from the pitch tracking data that tells us what ends up in the dirt and what doesn't. We also include a catcher's ability to prevent stolen bases and how well they field balls in play, and *finally* we come up with our FRAA for catchers.

Pitching

Both pitching and fielding make up the half of baseball that isn't run scoring: run prevention. Separating pitching from fielding is a tough task, and most recent pitching analysis has branched off from Voros McCracken's famous (and controversial) statement, "There is little if any difference among major-league pitchers in their ability to prevent hits on balls hit in the field of play." The research of the analytic community has validated this to some extent, and there are a host of "defense-independent" pitching measures that have been developed to try and extract the effect of the defense behind a hurler from the pitcher's work.

Our solution to this quandary is Deserved Run Average (DRA), our core pitching metric. DRA seeks to evaluate a pitcher's performance, much like earned run average (ERA), the tried-and-true pitching stat you've seen on every baseball broadcast or box score from the past century, but it's very different. To start, DRA takes an event-by-event look at what the pitchers does, and adjusts the value of that event based on different environmental factors like park, batter, catcher, umpire, base-out situation, run differential, inning, defense, home field advantage, pitcher role and temperature. That mixed model gives us a pitcher's expected contribution, similar to what we do for our DRC+ model for hitters and FRAA model for catchers. (Oh, and we also consider the pitcher's effect on basestealing and on balls getting past the catcher.)

DRA is set to the scale of runs allowed per nine innings (RA9) instead of ERA, which makes DRA's scale slightly higher than ERA's. Because of this, for ease of use, we're supplying DRA-, which is much easier for the reader to parse. As with DRC+, DRA- is an "index" stat, meaning instead of using some arbitrary and shifting number to denote what's "good," average is always 100. The reason that it uses a minus rather than a plus is because like ERA, a lower number is better. Therefore a 75 DRA- describes a performance 25 percent better than average, whereas a 150 DRA- means that either a pitcher is getting extremely lucky with their results, or getting ready to try a new pitch.

Since the last time you picked up an edition of this book, we've also made a few minor changes to DRA to make it better. Recent research into "tunneling"—the act of throwing consecutive pitches that appear similar from a batter's point of view until after the swing decision point–data has given us a new contextual factor to account for in DRA: plate distance. This refers to the distance between successive pitches as they approach the plate, and while it has a smaller effect than factors like velocity or whiff rate, it still can help explain pitcher strikeout rate in our model.

Recently Added Descriptive Statistics

Returning to our 2021 edition of the book are a few figures which recently appeared. These numbers may be a little bit more familiar to those of you who have spent some time investigating baseball statistics.

Fastball Percentage

Our fastball percentage (FA%) statistic measures how frequently a pitcher throws a pitch classified as a "fastball," measured as a percentage of overall pitches thrown. We qualify three types of fastballs:

1. The traditional four-seam fastball;
2. The two-seam fastball or sinker;
3. "Hard cutters," which are pitches that have the movement profile of a cut fastball and are used as the pitcher's primary offering or in place of a more traditional fastball.

For example, a pitcher with a FA% of 67 throws any combination of these three pitches about two-thirds of the time.

Whiff Rate

Everybody loves a swing and a miss, and whiff rate (Whiff%) measures how frequently pitchers induce a swinging strike. To calculate Whiff%, we add up all the pitches thrown that ended with a swinging strike, then divide that number by a pitcher's total pitches thrown. Most often, high whiff rates correlate with high strikeout rates (and overall effective pitcher performance).

Called Strike Probability

Called Strike Probability (CSP) is a number that represents the likelihood that all of a pitcher's pitches will be called a strike while controlling for location, pitcher and batter handedness, umpire and count. Here's how it works: on each pitch, our model determines how many times (out of 100) that a similar pitch was called for a strike given those factors mentioned above, and when normalized for each batter's strike zone. Then we average the CSP for all pitches thrown by a pitcher in a season, and that gives us the yearly CSP percentage you see in the stats boxes.

As you might imagine, pitchers with a higher CSP are more likely to work in the zone, where pitchers with a lower CSP are likely locating their pitches outside the normal strike zone, for better or for worse.

Projections

Many of you aren't turning to this book just for a look at what a player has done, but for a look at what a player is going to do: the PECOTA projections. PECOTA, initially developed by Nate Silver (who has moved on to greater fame as a political analyst), consists of three parts:

1. Major-league equivalencies, which use minor-league statistics to project how a player will perform in the major leagues;
2. Baseline forecasts, which use weighted averages and regression to the mean to estimate a player's current true talent level; and
3. Aging curves, which uses the career paths of comparable players to estimate how a player's statistics are likely to change over time.

With all those important things covered, let's take a look at what's in the book this year.

Team Prospectus

Most of this book is composed of team chapters, with one for each of the 30 major-league franchises. On the first page of each chapter, you'll see a box that contains some of the key statistics for each team as well as a very inviting stadium diagram.

We start with the team name, their unadjusted 2020 win-loss record, and their divisional ranking. Beneath that are a host of other team statistics. **Pythag** presents an adjusted 2020 winning percentage, calculated by taking runs scored per game (**RS/G**) and runs allowed per game (**RA/G**) for the team, and running them through a version of Bill James' Pythagorean formula that was refined and improved by David Smyth and Brandon Heipp. (The formula is called "Pythagenpat," which is equally fun to type and to say.)

Next up is **DRC+**, described earlier, to indicate the overall hitting ability of the team either above or below league-average. Run prevention on the pitching side is covered by **DRA** (also mentioned earlier) and another metric: Fielding Independent Pitching (**FIP**), which calculates another ERA-like statistic based on strikeouts, walks, and home runs recorded. Defensive Efficiency Rating (**DER**) tells us the percentage of balls in play turned into outs for the team, and is a quick fielding shorthand that rounds out run prevention.

After that, we have several measures related to roster composition, as opposed to on-field performance. **B-Age** and **P-Age** tell us the average age of a team's batters and pitchers, respectively. **Payroll** is the combined team payroll for all on-field players, and Doug Pappas' Marginal Dollars per Marginal Win (**M$/MW**) tells us how much money a team spent to earn production above replacement level.

Next to each of these stats, we've listed each team's MLB rank in that category from first to 30th. In this, first always indicates a positive outcome and 30th a negative outcome, except in the case of salary—first is highest.

After the franchise statistics, we share a few items about the team's home ballpark. There's the aforementioned diagram of the park's dimensions (including distances to the outfield wall), a graphic showing the height of the wall from the left-field pole to the right-field pole, and a table showing three-year park factors for the stadium. The park factors are displayed as indexes where 100 is average, 110 means that the park inflates the statistic in question by 10 percent, and 90 means that the park deflates the statistic in question by 10 percent.

On the second page of each team chapter, you'll find three graphs. The first is **Payroll History** and helps you see how the team's payroll has compared to the MLB and divisional average payrolls over time. Payroll figures are current as of January 1, 2021; with so many free agents still unsigned as of this writing, the final 2021 figure will likely be significantly different for many teams. (In the meantime, you can always find the most current data at Baseball Prospectus' Cot's Baseball Contracts page.)

The second graph is **Future Commitments** and helps you see the team's future outlays, if any.

The third graph is **Farm System Ranking** and displays how the Baseball Prospectus prospect team has ranked the organization's farm system since 2007.

After the graphs, we have a **Personnel** section that lists many of the important decision-makers and upper-level field and operations staff members for the franchise, as well as any former Baseball Prospectus staff members who are currently part of the organization. (In very rare circumstances, someone might be on both lists!)

Position Players

After all that information and a thoughtful bylined essay covering each team, we present our player comments. These are also bylined, but due to frequent franchise shifts during the offseason, our bylines are more a rough guide than a perfect accounting of who wrote what.

Each player is listed with the major-league team that employed him as of early January 2021. If a player changed teams after that point via free agency, trade, or any other method, you'll be able to find them in the chapter for their previous squad.

As an example, take a look at the player comment for Padres shortstop Fernando Tatis Jr.: the stat block that accompanies his written comment is at the top of this page. First we cover biographical information (age is as of June 30, 2021) before moving onto the stats themselves. Our statistic columns include standard identifying information like **YEAR**, **TEAM**, **LVL** (level of affiliated play) and **AGE** before getting into the numbers. Next, we provide raw, untranslated

Fernando Tatis Jr. SS
Born: 01/02/99   Age: 22   Bats: R   Throws: R
Height: 6'3"   Weight: 217   Origin: International Free Agent, 2015

YEAR	TEAM	LVL	AGE	PA	R	2B	3B	HR	RBI	BB	K	SB	CS	AVG/OBP/SLG
2018	SA	AA	19	394	77	22	4	16	43	33	109	16	5	.286/.355/.507
2019	SD	MLB	20	372	61	13	6	22	53	30	110	16	6	.317/.379/.590
2020	SD	MLB	21	257	50	11	2	17	45	27	61	11	3	.277/.366/.571
2021 FS	SD	MLB	22	600	95	24	4	31	81	50	165	17	8	.263/.331/.499
2021 DC	SD	MLB	22	628	100	25	4	32	85	53	173	19	8	.263/.331/.499

Comparables: Darryl Strawberry, Bo Bichette, Ronald Acuña Jr.

YEAR	TEAM	LVL	AGE	PA	DRC+	BABIP	BRR	FRAA	WARP
2018	SA	AA	19	394	136	.370	3.0	SS(83): -1.9	2.4
2019	SD	MLB	20	372	118	.410	7.1	SS(83): 0.9	3.4
2020	SD	MLB	21	257	126	.306	0.7	SS(57): -5.5	0.9
2021 FS	SD	MLB	22	600	126	.318	1.7	SS -1	3.9
2021 DC	SD	MLB	22	628	126	.318	1.8	SS -1	4.0

numbers like you might find on the back of your dad's baseball cards: **PA** (plate appearances), **R** (runs), **2B** (doubles), **3B** (triples), **HR** (home runs), **RBI** (runs batted in), **BB** (walks), **K** (strikeouts), **SB** (stolen bases) and **CS** (caught stealing).

Following the basic stats is **Whiff%** (whiff rate), which denotes how often, when a batter swings, he fails to make contact with the ball. Another way to think of this number is an inverse of a hitter's contact rate.

Next, we have unadjusted "slash" statistics: **AVG** (batting average), **OBP** (on-base percentage) and **SLG** (slugging percentage). Following the slash line is **DRC+** (Deserved Runs Created Plus), which we described earlier as total offensive expected contribution compared to the league average.

BABIP (batting average on balls in play) tells us how often a ball in play fell for a hit, and can help us identify whether a batter may have been lucky or not ... but note that high BABIPs also tend to follow the great hitters of our time, as well as speedy singles hitters who put the ball on the ground.

The next item is **BRR** (Baserunning Runs), which covers all of a player's baserunning accomplishments including (but not limited to) swiped bags and failed attempts. Next is **FRAA** (Fielding Runs Above Average), which also includes the number of games previously played at each position noted in parentheses. Multi-position players have only their two most frequent positions listed here, but their total FRAA number reflects all positions played.

Our last column here is **WARP** (Wins Above Replacement Player). WARP estimates the total value of a player, which means for hitters it takes into account hitting runs above average (calculated using the DRC+ model), BRR and FRAA. Then, it makes an adjustment for positions played and gives the player a credit for plate appearances based upon the difference between "replacement level"—which is derived from the quality of players added to a team's roster after the start of the season–and the league average.

The final line just below the stats box is **PECOTA** data, which is discussed further in a following section.

Catchers

Catchers are a special breed, and thus they have earned their own separate box which displays some of the defensive metrics that we've built just for them. As an example, let's check out Yasmani Grandal.

YEAR	TEAM	P. COUNT	FRM RUNS	BLK RUNS	THRW RUNS	TOT RUNS
2018	LAD	16816	15.7	0.8	0.1	16.5
2019	MIL	18740	19.4	1.8	-0.1	21.1
2020	CHW	4830	3.7	0.3	-0.2	3.8
2021	CHW	14430	16.7	-0.6	1.0	17.1
2021	CHW	14430	16.7	0.4	1.0	18.0

The **YEAR** and **TEAM** columns match what you'd find in the other stat box. **P. COUNT** indicates the number of pitches thrown while the catcher was behind the plate, including swinging strikes, fouls and balls in play. **FRM RUNS** is the total run value the catcher provided (or cost) his team by influencing the umpire to call strikes where other catchers did not. **BLK RUNS** expresses the total run value above or below average for the catcher's ability to prevent wild pitches and passed balls. **THRW RUNS** is calculated using a similar model as the previous two statistics, and it measures a catcher's ability to throw out basestealers but also to dissuade them from testing his arm in the first place. It takes into account factors like the pitcher (including his delivery and pickoff move) and baserunner (who could be as fast as Billy Hamilton or as slow as Yonder Alonso). **TOT RUNS** is the sum of all of the previous three statistics.

Pitchers

Let's give our pitchers a turn, using 2020 AL Cy Young winner Shane Bieber as our example. Take a look at his stat block: the first line and the **YEAR**, **TEAM**, **LVL** and **AGE** columns are the same as in the position player example earlier.

Here too, we have a series of columns that display raw, unadjusted statistics compiled by the pitcher over the course of a season: **W** (wins), **L** (losses), **SV** (saves), **G** (games pitched), **GS** (games started), **IP** (innings pitched), **H** (hits allowed) and **HR** (home runs allowed). Next we have two statistics that are rates: **BB/9** (walks per nine innings) and **K/9** (strikeouts per nine innings), before returning to the unadjusted K (strikeouts).

Next up is **GB%** (ground ball percentage), which is the percentage of all batted balls that were hit on the ground, including both outs and hits. Remember, this is based on observational data and subject to human error, so please approach this with a healthy dose of skepticism.

BABIP (batting average on balls in play) is calculated using the same methodology as it is for position players, but it often tells us more about a pitcher than it does a hitter. With pitchers, a high BABIP is often due to poor defense or bad luck, and can often be an indicator of potential rebound, and a low BABIP may be cause to expect performance regression. (A typical league-average BABIP is close to .290-.300.)

The metrics **WHIP** (walks plus hits per inning pitched) and **ERA** (earned run average) are old standbys: WHIP measures walks and hits allowed on a per-inning basis, while ERA measures earned runs on a nine-inning basis. Neither of these stats are translated or adjusted.

DRA- (Deserved Run Average) was described at length earlier, and measures how the pitcher "deserved" to perform compared to other pitchers. Please note that since we lack all the data points that would make for a "real" DRA for minor-league events, the DRA- displayed for minor league partial-seasons is based off of different data. (That data is a modified version of our cFIP metric, which you can find more information about on our website.)

Shane Bieber   RHP

Born: 05/31/95   Age: 26   Bats: R   Throws: R
Height: 6'3"   Weight: 200   Origin: Round 4, 2016 Draft (#122 overall)

YEAR	TEAM	LVL	AGE	W	L	SV	G	GS	IP	H	HR	BB/9	K/9	K	GB%	BABIP
2018	AKR	AA	23	3	0	0	5	5	31	26	1	0.3	8.7	30	47.3%	.278
2018	COL	AAA	23	3	1	0	8	8	48[2]	30	3	1.1	8.7	47	52.0%	.227
2018	CLE	MLB	23	11	5	0	20	19	114[2]	130	13	1.8	9.3	118	46.2%	.356
2019	CLE	MLB	24	15	8	0	34	33	214[1]	186	31	1.7	10.9	259	44.4%	.298
2020	CLE	MLB	25	8	1	0	12	12	77[1]	46	7	2.4	14.2	122	48.4%	.267
2021 FS	CLE	MLB	26	10	6	0	26	26	150	121	18	2.1	11.7	195	45.5%	.297
2021 DC	CLE	MLB	26	14	7	0	30	30	196.7	159	24	2.1	11.7	257	45.5%	.297

Comparables: Luis Severino, Danny Salazar, Joe Musgrove

YEAR	TEAM	LVL	AGE	WHIP	ERA	DRA-	WARP	MPH	FB%	WHF	CSP
2018	AKR	AA	23	0.87	1.16	61	0.9				
2018	COL	AAA	23	0.74	1.66	69	1.2				
2018	CLE	MLB	23	1.33	4.55	74	2.6	94.7	57.4%	26.2%	
2019	CLE	MLB	24	1.05	3.28	75	4.9	94.4	45.8%	30.8%	
2020	CLE	MLB	25	0.87	1.63	53	2.6	95.3	53.6%	40.7%	
2021 FS	CLE	MLB	26	1.04	2.44	64	4.4	94.7	50.0%	33.2%	44.2%
2021 DC	CLE	MLB	26	1.04	2.44	64	5.8	94.7	50.0%	33.2%	44.2%

Just like with hitters, **WARP** (Wins Above Replacement Player) is a total value metric that puts pitchers of all stripes on the same scale as position players. We use DRA as the primary input for our calculation of WARP. You might notice that relief pitchers (due to their limited innings) may have a lower WARP than you were expecting or than you might see in other WARP-like metrics. WARP does not take leverage into account, just the actions a pitcher performs and the expected value of those actions ... which ends up judging high-leverage relief pitchers differently than you might imagine given their prestige and market value.

MPH gives you the pitcher's 95th percentile velocity for the noted season, in order to give you an idea of what the *peak* fastball velocity a pitcher possesses. Since this comes from our pitch-tracking data, it is not publicly available for minor-league pitchers.

Finally, we display the three new pitching metrics we described earlier. **FB%** (fastball percentage) gives you the percentage of fastballs thrown out of all pitches. **WHF** (whiff rate) tells you the percentage of swinging strikes induced out of all pitches. **CSP** (called strike probability) expresses the likelihood of all pitches thrown to result in a called strike, after controlling for factors like handedness, umpire, pitch type, count and location.

PECOTA

All players have PECOTA projections for 2021, as well as a set of other numbers that describe the performance of comparable players according to PECOTA. All projections for 2021 are for the player at the date we went to press in early January and are projected into the league and park context as indicated by the team abbreviation. (Note that players at very low levels of the minors are too unpredictable to assess using these numbers.) All PECOTA projected statistics represent a player's projected major-league performance.

How we're doing that is a little different this season. There are really two different values that go into the final stat line that you see for PECOTA: How a player performs, and how much playing time he'll be given to perform it. In the past we've estimated playing time based on each team's roster and depth charts, and we'll continue to do that. These projections are denoted as **2021 DC**.

But in many cases, a player won't be projected for major-league playing time; most of the time this is because they aren't projected to be major-league players at all, but still developing as prospects. Or perhaps a player will provide Triple-A depth, only to have an opportunity open up because of injury. For these purposes, we're also supplying a second projection, labeled **2021 FS**, or full season. This is what we would project the player to provide in 600 plate appearances or 150 innings pitched.

Below the projections are the player's three highest-scoring comparable players as determined by PECOTA. All comparables represent a snapshot of how the listed player was performing at the same age as the current player, so if a

23-year-old pitcher is compared to Bartolo Colón, he's actually being compared to a 23-year-old Colón, not the version that pitched for the Rangers in 2018, nor to Colón's career as a whole.

A few points about pitcher projections. First, we aren't yet projecting peak velocity, so that column will be blank in the PECOTA lines. Second, projecting DRA is trickier than evaluating past performance, because it is unclear how deserving each pitcher will be of his anticipated outcomes. However, we know that another DRA-related statistic–contextual FIP or cFIP-estimates future run scoring very well. So for PECOTA, the projected DRA- figures you see are based on the past cFIPs generated by the pitcher and comparable players over time, along with the other factors described above.

If you're familiar with PECOTA, then you'll have noticed that the projection system often appears bullish on players coming off a bad year and bearish on players coming off a good year. (This is because the system weights several previous seasons, not just the most recent one.) In addition, we publish the 50th percentile projections for each player–which is smack in the middle of the range of projected production—which tends to mean PECOTA stat lines don't often have extreme results like 40 home runs or 250 strikeouts in a given season. In essence, PECOTA doesn't project very many extreme seasons.

Managers

After all those wonderful team chapters, we've got statistics for each big-league manager, all of whom are organized by alphabetical order. Here you'll find a block including an extraordinary amount of information collected from each manager's entire career. For more information on the acronyms and what they mean, please visit the Glossary at www.baseballprospectus.com.

There is one important metric that we'd like to call attention to, and you'll find it next to each manager's name: **wRM+** (weighted reliever management plus). Developed by Rob Arthur and Rian Watt, wRM+ investigates how good a manager is at using their best relievers during the moments of highest leverage, using both our proprietary DRA metric as well as Leverage Index. wRM+ is scaled to a league average of 100, and a wRM+ of 105 indicates that relievers were used approximately five percent "better" than average. On the other hand, a wRM+ of 95 would tell us the team used its relievers five percent "worse" than the average team.

While wRM+ does not have an extremely strong correlation with a manager, it is statistically significant; this means that a manager is not *entirely* responsible for a team's wRM+, but does have some effect on that number.

Part 1: Team Analysis

Performance Graphs

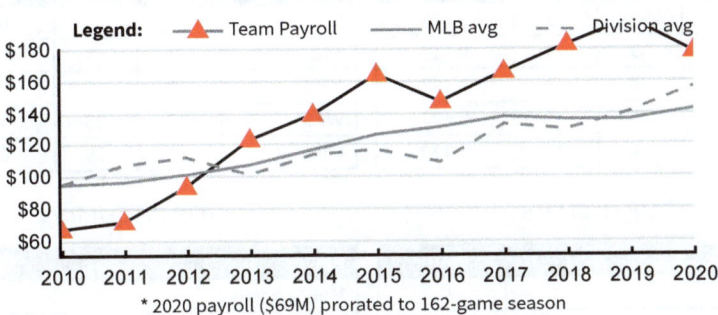

*2020 payroll ($69M) prorated to 162-game season

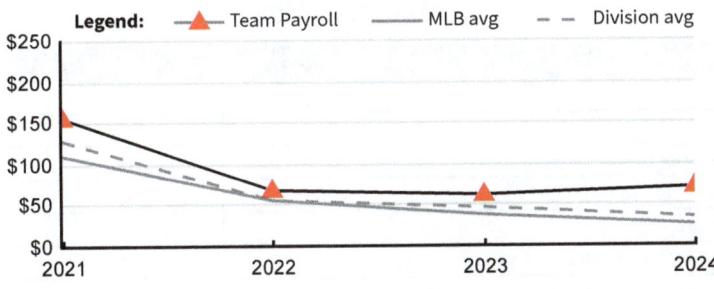

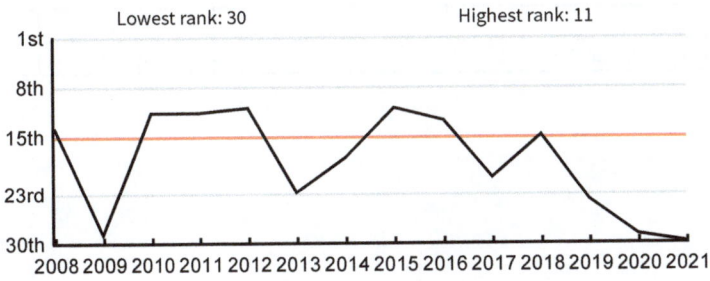

2020 Team Performance

ACTUAL STANDINGS

Team	W	L	Pct
ATL	35	25	0.583
MIA	31	29	0.517
PHI	28	32	0.467
NYM	26	34	0.433
WAS	**26**	**34**	**0.433**

dWIN% STANDINGS

Team	W	L	Pct
PHI	34	26	0.580
ATL	33	27	0.562
NYM	32	28	0.549
WAS	**27**	**33**	**0.450**
MIA	25	35	0.431

TOP HITTERS

Player	WARP
Juan Soto	1.6
Trea Turner	1.5
Carter Kieboom	0.5

TOP PITCHERS

Player	WARP
Max Scherzer	1.3
Patrick Corbin	0.6
Tanner Rainey	0.4

VITAL STATISTICS

Statistic Name	Value	Rank
Pythagenpat	.487	16th
dWin%	.450	18th
Runs Scored per Game	4.88	10th
Runs Allowed per Game	5.02	20th
Deserved Runs Created Plus	103	11th
Deserved Run Average Minus	123	30th
Fielding Independent Pitching	5.06	27th
Defensive Efficiency Rating	.667	28th
Batter Age	29.1	26th
Pitcher Age	31.4	30th
Payroll	$69.0M	8th
Marginal $ per Marginal Win	$6.4M	26th

2021 Team Projections

PROJECTED STANDINGS

Team	W	L	Pct	+/-
NYM	93.6	68.4	0.578	23
Their additions should yield the best Mets team since 2015, even if their competition in the NL East is much stiffer than it was then.				
WAS	84.7	77.3	0.523	14
Mike Rizzo remade the middle of his lineup and improved the pitching staff, but given the caliber of their competition he could have aimed a hair higher.				
PHI	83.8	78.2	0.517	8
Re-signing J.T. Realmuto and Didi Gregorius keeps the offense intact, but has Dave Dombrowski successfully built a bullpen?				
ATL	81.5	80.5	0.503	-13
The rotation and positional stars set a high floor; their role players will determine their ceiling.				
MIA	70.9	91.1	0.438	-12
Hired a transformational leader and then did nothing to improve (or even reshape) a middling roster.				

TOP PROJECTED HITTERS

Player	WARP
Juan Soto	6.5
Trea Turner	5.0
Kyle Schwarber	3.0

TOP PROJECTED PITCHERS

Player	WARP
Max Scherzer	4.6
Stephen Strasburg	3.1
Patrick Corbin	2.4

FARM SYSTEM REPORT

Top Prospect	Number of Top 101 Prospects
Cade Cavalli	0

KEY DEDUCTIONS

Player	WARP
Adam Eaton	1.6
Sean Doolittle	0.9
Michael A. Taylor	0.4
Kurt Suzuki	0.3

KEY ADDITIONS

Player	WARP
Kyle Schwarber	3.0
Josh Bell	1.6
Jon Lester	1.0
Brad Hand	0.8
Joe Ross	0.4
Rogelio Armenteros	0.3

Team Personnel

General Manager & President of Baseball Operations
Mike Rizzo

Assistant General Manager & Vice President, Player Personnel
Doug Harris

Assistant General Manager & Vice President, Scouting Operations
Kris Kline

Assistant General Manager, Baseball Operations
Michael DeBartolo

Manager
Dave Martinez

Nationals Park Stats

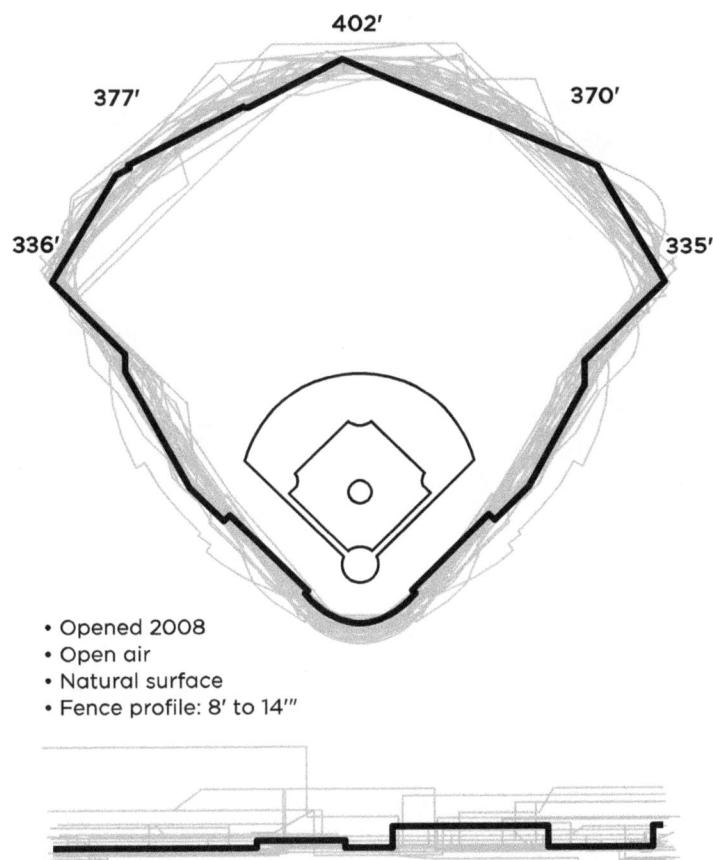

- Opened 2008
- Open air
- Natural surface
- Fence profile: 8' to 14'"

Three-Year Park Factors

Runs	Runs/RH	Runs/LH	HR/RH	HR/LH
104	104	105	108	107

Nationals Team Analysis

The year 2021 marks the beginning of the rest of Washington Nationals fans' lives.

When the team first arrived at RFK Stadium back in the day, they delivered an improbable 81-81 record, with manager Frank Robinson at the helm and Vinny Castilla at third base. The team's lodging under that sagging halo allowed them to capitalize on the nostalgia from the franchises that played there before, and when they moved into Nationals Park, fandom became an odd process of self-identification in the nation's capital.

People didn't demand culture, they just wanted to see baseball in a new park, eat some hot dogs and catch some organ music, but the team was bad. Unwatchably bad. Sure, Mr. National Ryan Zimmerman plugged along, and we got fan favorites like Chad Cordero, Dmitri Young and personal fav Ronnie Beliiard. But until they got back-to-back top picks in the draft, and hauled in Strasburg and Harper (and Rendon the year after at number six), it was a wasteland, best defined by the time the team took the field wearing jerseys missing a letter, reading "Natinals" instead of Nationals. The vibe fit.

When Zim went yard to inaugurate the new stadium on Sunday Night Baseball remains the greatest moment in franchise history, but those achievements occurred amidst consecutive 100-loss seasons. In a lot of ways, he was the facelessness of the franchise. When a hot first half landed him an All-Star berth in 2017, everyone realized: That was only his *second*? One Gold Glove, no Top-10 MVP finishes? All that greatness, just vanished with the newsprint.

Then, the organization was sprinkled with a little stardust that changed the trajectory of the franchise.

It served as a headfirst dive into How To Build A Baseball Town 101. They drafted Stephen Strasburg and his development was A1 news from the jump. The fans who dug themselves into the trenches of the Nationals internet circles were people who paid close attention to his ins and outs, because that was the only way to care about baseball in D.C. What the Nationals provided for many in the area, was a local sports team that didn't demand a lot of travel. Locals either had renounced fandom after the Senators left, or had latched on to the Orioles and were switching over. The new team felt like it was wedged in between the Orioles and Braves. Because the Nats were so new, there was something of an expectations-free ease to the fandom, at least until Strasburg arrived in the big leagues.

Washington Nationals 2021

Strasmas was real. His debut was televised nationally: a Tuesday night game against the Pirates at Nationals Park, the night before the anniversary of his selection in the draft. Seven innings. Two runs. Fourteen strikeouts and zero walks. The Pirates may as well have been the Washington Generals. Grown folks who'd spent a lot of time being extremely rational about a young man making his way to the bigs were suddenly agog, rightfully so, after one start. The whole beginning of his career led to a level of high-volume feelings that are almost too intense to revisit in detail.

Tommy John. The "shutdown." Inverted W's. It was like watching your kid take dishes out of the dishwasher. For something so early in the franchise's history, it was one of the more exhausting exercises in team support, even for the most intense baseball fans, much less ones who had gravitated towards the team in a low-stakes environment. Fandom didn't mean rooting for the team, it meant having an opinion on it. The feel-good, show-up-and-watch-a-game era was over. All of a sudden you had to pick a side. It was annoying.

Point being, everyone got to learn how much they were going to care, long before the team started contending. Those years fans spend investing, soaking it in, getting used to the idea of caring, all came crashing down in a single wave. Everything that had to happen, did. They signed Jayson Werth to a deal that people knew was likely to be overvalued in terms of money, but if that's what it took to land him, so be it. And to an extent, it worked. Random free agent veteran to bring attitude and leadership and energy to the team just like in the movies? Check.

Bryce Harper, Rookie of the Century comes along, wins Rookie of the Year, they make the playoffs, Davey Johnson won Manager of the Year award and three separate guys won Silver Slugger (including Strasburg).

Okay now it's time to start winning.

Don't hold your breath. They lost to the Cardinals that year. The next year Bryce Harper won seemingly every award known to humankind and they didn't even make the playoffs. Whatever, it was a fun year!

Okay, NOW it's time to start winning?

The next year, Daniel Murphy showed up, Anthony Rendon was a beacon, and Max Scherzer won the Cy Young Award two years after signing an eye-popping $210M contract.

Surely, now it was REALLY time to start winning, no?

No. They lost to the Dodgers in the NLDS.

By this point, we've had enough case law to show the many different facets of Nats fans. The ones who think this team's cheapness with managers is coming back to haunt them. The ones who buy into some absurd curse for shutting down Stras back when they thought the team really had a chance to win something years back, god knows what. The fan base was officially self-identifying as "short-suffering." The idea being that even if the team wasn't, say, the Cubs, the nature of the collapses was no less devastating, considering the circumstances. Some Cleveland fan might say they'd been suffering for 70 years and be 25 years old. Time wipes away the old pain, but in terms of new pain, no one had Nats fans beat. It's a "what have you done to me lately" mentality, and it leaves scars. Shit, Pete Kozma showed up in the Australian League world series a couple seasons back and I instantly got tight about it.

The honeymoon period was over. They'd thrown too much money around, received too much love and were too well-liked for the "aw shucks our guys didn't get it done this year" stuff to work. 2017 suddenly became a sort of understated World Series or bust year, and Scherzer won the Cy Young Award AGAIN. They won the division by 20 games.

NOW, IT IS DEFINITELY TIME TO F***ING WIN SOMETHING.

They didn't make it out of the NLDS.

The images of Willson Contreras backpicking guys all series, eventually ending the best threat the Nationals had to take the series is still burned in this author's brain. Dusty Baker, a surefire Hall of Famer and previous Manager of the Year (three times!) was shown the door. The franchise had gone from teenage youthful enthusiasm to grown-man grizzled goonery in the time it took for Jose Lobaton's ankle to flex, straighten, and then return to the bag (he was safe, by the way).

They didn't even make the playoffs the next year. They missed the postseason with a manager who thought bringing camels to spring training was a good idea, to you know, get over the hump. I'm sure it sounded good on paper. The Nationals were now officially a bit of a circus. Honestly, they got bailed out because the Capitals, a team that spent its own 40 days in the desert, won the Stanley Cup and the catharsis was so intense nobody cared about anything for the rest of the year.

Then 2019 happened. Bryce Harper, once the past, present and future was gone to Philly. After a godawful start that we all remember, they actually won the whole damn thing. Not exactly out of nowhere, but certainly not expected the way things started. It was as if they'd broken the pattern. As Strasburg, the World Series MVP, himself said, "sometimes you're the buzzsaw." Somehow Gerardo Parra's walkup song "Baby Shark" became the theme of the season, after the veteran landed with the Nats about a week after the Giants released him. Fourth outfielders are supposed to, on some level, be good clubhouse presences, but they're not supposed to win over an entire fanbase. When they won it was surreal, to say the least.

Then, before the next season even got started, a pandemic broke out, and suddenly the Nationals championship victory lap was cut short. Of course, the 2020 season did eventually happen. But at that point, a team that had literally built itself from the ground up was a shell of itself. The magic had worn off guys like Aníbal Sánchez and Howie Kendrick, who just looked old. Zimmerman opted out entirely and Strasburg shut it down early with a hand injury.

After literal generations without a team, a decade plus of well-earned heartbreak and then a completely insane title run, we only had ourselves to really celebrate it with. Literally, inside of our homes. The season after a championship is supposed to be one long parade: Disappointing season? Blame it on the hangover from the champagne. But the time off was long enough for everyone to sober up, and 2020 became more like cleaning up the plastic cups after a house party.

Why does all that matter? Because the Nationals have an identity to sort out. They're no longer the plucky new kids. They're no longer the kinda embarrassing middle schoolers. They're far from the overly cocky high school kids who thought their whole lives were ahead of them. We've moved past the existential dread of disappointment through repeated failure. They won the World Series! Then we all forgot about everything.

The main question becomes what is acceptable from a year-to-year standpoint. Are they going to do that thing where they act like "Champion" is their only identity? Are they going to hit reset and start the whole thing over, go back to the early Zimmerman days? Or are they going to be who they should be, and just continue to grow and build the game from a fan standpoint?

When pitchers and catchers report to West Palm Beach in 2021, the Nationals will be back to being just another team, oddly enough. A decent team, a longshot, but a shot. The team has their trophy, and we got our parade, but we missed the victory lap—the season-long celebration of each other, of the investment everyone made.

The MLS' Seattle Sounders were technically the last team awarded a trophy before it all came down, but it wasn't that franchise's first time. This was different. And as we came to find out, the Nats beat a team of cheats. In many ways, they kind of saved baseball, nevermind themselves. If you thought MLB was under the microscope following the revelation that the Astros had a coordinated sign-stealing scheme, think about the level of scandal it would be if they'd just claimed their second title in three seasons. There was no saving baseball, or any sport, from the fire that was a worldwide pandemic, but the Nationals pulled MLB out of the frying pan it almost found itself in. But the fact of the matter is that the 2019 Nationals will probably never get the credit they deserve. Fans will only get over that if the franchise does too. What fans expect or even want from this team in 2021, nevermind the franchise going forward, will be fascinating to see.

Luckily, there is one person that every Nationals fan can throw all their efforts toward. Not merely a star—stars litter the night's sky—the man they call Childish Bambino is the Nationals' sun; as long as he's in their orbit, there will be light. Already a champion, Juan Soto is the past, the present and the future.

—Clinton Yates is a columnist for The Undefeated and panelist on Around The Horn.

Part 2: Player Analysis

PLAYER COMMENTS WITH GRAPHS

Josh Bell 1B
Born: 08/14/92   Age: 28   Bats: S   Throws: R
Height: 6'4"   Weight: 250   Origin: Round 2, 2011 Draft (#61 overall)

YEAR	TEAM	LVL	AGE	PA	R	2B	3B	HR	RBI	BB	K	SB	CS	AVG/OBP/SLG
2018	PIT	MLB	25	583	74	31	4	12	62	77	104	2	5	.261/.357/.411
2019	PIT	MLB	26	613	94	37	3	37	116	74	118	0	1	.277/.367/.569
2020	PIT	MLB	27	223	22	3	0	8	22	22	59	0	0	.226/.305/.364
2021 FS	WAS	MLB	28	600	81	26	2	23	84	70	140	2	2	.246/.338/.442
2021 DC	WAS	MLB	28	554	75	24	2	21	78	64	129	1	2	.246/.338/.442

Comparables: Logan Morrison, Lucas Duda, Derrek Lee

Bell is built like a hybrid of Optimus Prime and an old-growth sequoia, so it's frustrating the power has been just average. It looked like a power surge was coming in 2019, when he dialed up his launch angle and started barreling the ball more, swinging more often at pitches in the zone while smoothing out an idiosyncratic approach at the plate. That method regressed in 2020, as he continued to swing at strikes but also swung through them, costing him the hit tool that was his calling card throughout the minors. A defensive liability even at first, without a universal DH it's hard to find a place for him, and he's still got two more years before free agency. That primed the pump for a trade to the Nationals, where he will try to rediscover his power stroke from 2019.

YEAR	TEAM	LVL	AGE	PA	DRC+	BABIP	BRR	FRAA	WARP
2018	PIT	MLB	25	583	100	.305	-0.8	1B(137): -6.8	0.1
2019	PIT	MLB	26	613	130	.288	-3.1	1B(134): -11.1	2.0
2020	PIT	MLB	27	223	83	.273	-0.4	1B(35): -0.0	-0.1
2021 FS	WAS	MLB	28	600	114	.291	-0.6	1B -2	1.7
2021 DC	WAS	MLB	28	554	114	.291	-0.5	1B -2	1.6

Josh Bell, continued

Batted Ball Distribution

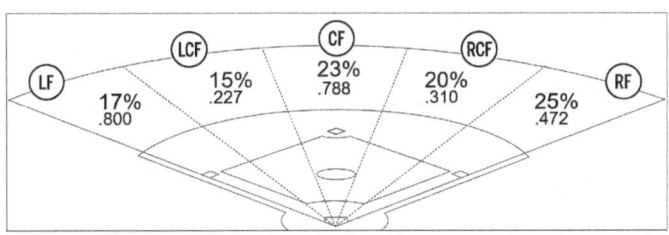

Strike Zone vs LHP **Strike Zone vs RHP**

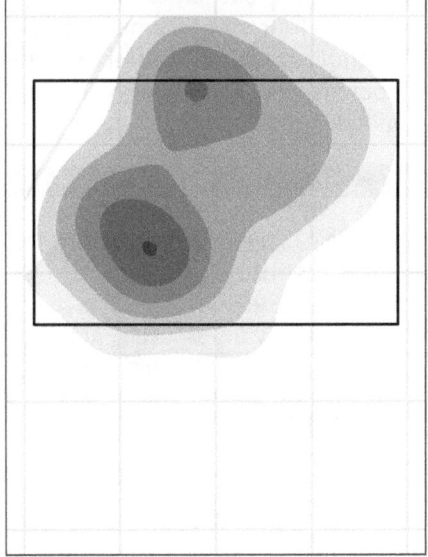

Asdrúbal Cabrera 3B

Born: 11/13/85   Age: 35   Bats: S   Throws: R
Height: 6'0"   Weight: 205   Origin: International Free Agent, 2002

YEAR	TEAM	LVL	AGE	PA	R	2B	3B	HR	RBI	BB	K	SB	CS	AVG/OBP/SLG
2018	PHI	MLB	32	185	20	13	0	5	17	12	38	0	0	.228/.286/.392
2018	NYM	MLB	32	407	48	23	1	18	58	29	81	0	0	.277/.329/.488
2019	WAS	MLB	33	146	24	10	1	6	40	19	18	0	0	.323/.404/.565
2019	TEX	MLB	33	368	45	15	0	12	51	38	85	4	0	.235/.318/.393
2020	WAS	MLB	34	213	23	9	3	8	31	19	39	0	0	.242/.305/.447
2021 FS	WAS	MLB	35	600	64	25	1	19	69	49	128	3	1	.244/.312/.401
2021 DC	WAS	MLB	35	237	25	10	0	7	27	19	50	0	1	.244/.312/.401

Comparables: Jhonny Peralta, J.J. Hardy, Rich Aurilia

The Nationals found treasure in the scrapheap in 2019, signing Cabrera for a paltry sum after his release from the Rangers and receiving All-Star production from him during the run up to the postseason. Like the Nationals, he failed to repeat the same kind of magic last season, putting up numbers more similar to the ones he posted in Texas. The only glimmers of good fortune present in his season came versus lefties (against whom he put up an OPS above 1.000), and three of the four other members of the NL East. (He was, improbably, stymied by Philadelphia pitching.) Cabrera's competence against southpaws, combined with defensive versatility, should ensure him at least another season as a back-up infielder.

YEAR	TEAM	LVL	AGE	PA	DRC+	BABIP	BRR	FRAA	WARP
2018	PHI	MLB	32	185	107	.266	0.5	SS(31): -0.6, 3B(22): -0.5, 2B(2): 0.1	0.8
2018	NYM	MLB	32	407	104	.309	1.9	2B(90): -10.8	0.6
2019	WAS	MLB	33	146	137	.330	-1.2	2B(31): -1.6, 3B(5): -0.3, 1B(3): 0.3	0.9
2019	TEX	MLB	33	368	94	.278	0.2	3B(93): 6.0	1.8
2020	WAS	MLB	34	213	103	.259	0.5	1B(25): -0.9, 3B(17): -1.3	0.3
2021 FS	WAS	MLB	35	600	96	.285	-0.6	2B -2, 3B 0	0.9
2021 DC	WAS	MLB	35	237	96	.285	-0.2	2B -1, 3B 0	0.3

Asdrúbal Cabrera, continued

Batted Ball Distribution

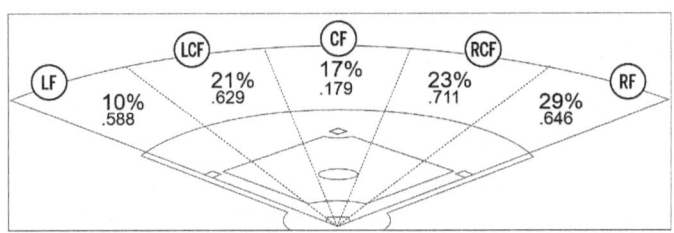

Strike Zone vs LHP   **Strike Zone vs RHP**

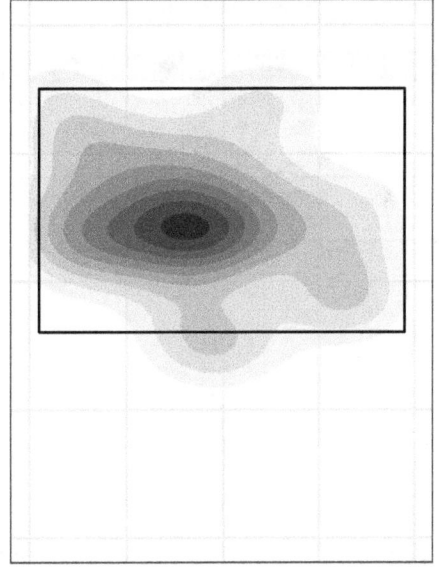

Starlin Castro 2B

Born: 03/24/90 Age: 31 Bats: R Throws: R
Height: 6'2" Weight: 220 Origin: International Free Agent, 2006

YEAR	TEAM	LVL	AGE	PA	R	2B	3B	HR	RBI	BB	K	SB	CS	AVG/OBP/SLG
2018	MIA	MLB	28	647	76	32	2	12	54	48	124	6	4	.278/.329/.400
2019	MIA	MLB	29	676	68	31	4	22	86	28	111	2	2	.270/.300/.436
2020	WAS	MLB	30	63	9	3	1	2	4	3	13	0	0	.267/.302/.450
2021 FS	WAS	MLB	31	600	74	26	1	18	75	32	126	3	2	.260/.303/.412
2021 DC	WAS	MLB	31	568	70	24	1	17	71	30	119	2	2	.260/.303/.412

Comparables: Mike Aviles, Jordy Mercer, Ian Desmond

It's not the years; it's the miles. Castro will be entering his 11th season in the bigs, with almost 1,500 games—including a pair of 162-appearance seasons—to show for his efforts. Despite being on the younger side (especially in an aging Nationals lineup), there isn't much intrigue left here. Castro's best skill is, arguably, his durability—or, at least, it *was,* until he suffered a fractured wrist on a diving attempt a few weeks into the season. Heading forward, he should continue to hit decently, walk infrequently and—most importantly of all—be available almost every day.

YEAR	TEAM	LVL	AGE	PA	DRC+	BABIP	BRR	FRAA	WARP
2018	MIA	MLB	28	647	101	.330	0.3	2B(150): -6.2	1.6
2019	MIA	MLB	29	676	90	.293	-1.8	2B(117): -6.2, 3B(45): -0.3, SS(3): -0.2	0.6
2020	WAS	MLB	30	63	103	.311	-0.3	2B(16): 0.2	0.2
2021 FS	WAS	MLB	31	600	95	.305	-0.5	2B -3, 3B 0	1.0
2021 DC	WAS	MLB	31	568	95	.305	-0.5	2B -3	1.0

Starlin Castro, continued

Batted Ball Distribution

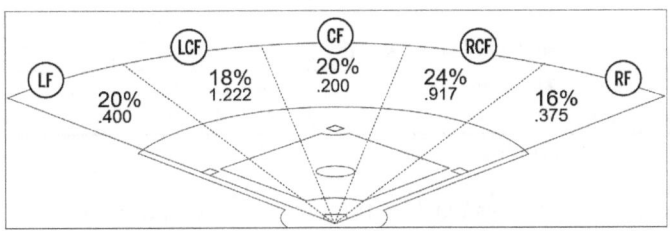

Strike Zone vs LHP   ### Strike Zone vs RHP

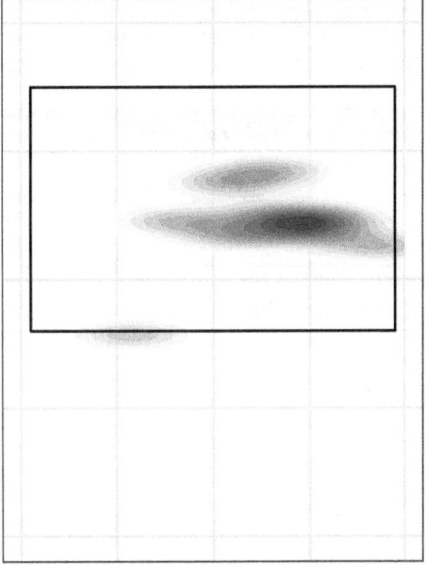

Washington Nationals 2021

Luis García SS
Born: 05/16/00   Age: 21   Bats: L   Throws: R
Height: 6'2"   Weight: 211   Origin: International Free Agent, 2016

YEAR	TEAM	LVL	AGE	PA	R	2B	3B	HR	RBI	BB	K	SB	CS	AVG/OBP/SLG
2018	HAG	LO-A	18	323	48	14	4	3	31	19	49	8	5	.297/.335/.402
2018	FBG	HI-A	18	221	34	7	2	4	23	12	33	4	1	.299/.338/.412
2019	HBG	AA	19	553	66	22	4	4	30	17	86	11	5	.257/.280/.337
2020	WAS	MLB	20	139	18	6	0	2	16	5	29	1	1	.276/.302/.366
2021 FS	WAS	MLB	21	600	59	26	3	9	64	22	133	5	3	.250/.281/.356
2021 DC	WAS	MLB	21	224	22	9	1	3	23	8	49	2	1	.250/.281/.356

Comparables: Ramiro Pena, Elvis Andrus, Rubén Tejada

Garcia has a good claim as Washington's top prospect, though that's in a system so thin you can practically see through it. Regardless, he has a solid hit tool and should grow into his power (he didn't turn 20 until May). While shortstop may ultimately be too tough for him, he'll find a comfortable home at second base. He even managed to hold his own in a brief MLB stint, though walking just five times in 40 games suggests there's more work to do. Garcia should keep developing in Triple-A to begin 2021, and then take over the keystone in D.C. when he's ready, maybe around June. "Soon," Nationals fans whisper, casting a worried glance at Starlin Castro and Carter Kieboom.

YEAR	TEAM	LVL	AGE	PA	DRC+	BABIP	BRR	FRAA	WARP
2018	HAG	LO-A	18	323	109	.343	0.7	3B(36): -4.6, SS(27): 0.4, 2B(11): -1.2	0.4
2018	FBG	HI-A	18	221	115	.337	-0.3	SS(40): -2.7	0.4
2019	HBG	AA	19	553	69	.299	3.1	SS(93): -3.9, 2B(38): 0.4	0.5
2020	WAS	MLB	20	139	64	.340	-0.8	2B(37): -11.3, SS(3): 0.0	-1.4
2021 FS	WAS	MLB	21	600	71	.312	0.1	SS 0, 2B -5	-1.1
2021 DC	WAS	MLB	21	224	71	.312	0.0	SS 0, 2B -2	-0.4

Luis García, continued

Batted Ball Distribution

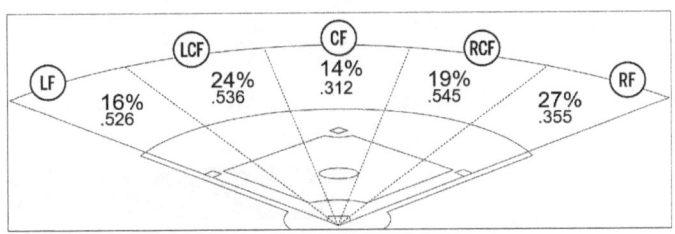

Strike Zone vs LHP   **Strike Zone vs RHP**

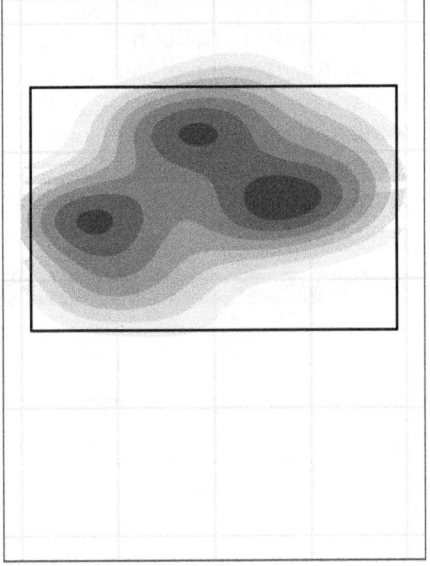

Yan Gomes C

Born: 07/19/87   Age: 33   Bats: R   Throws: R
Height: 6'2"   Weight: 215   Origin: Round 10, 2009 Draft (#310 overall)

YEAR	TEAM	LVL	AGE	PA	R	2B	3B	HR	RBI	BB	K	SB	CS	AVG/OBP/SLG
2018	CLE	MLB	30	435	52	26	0	16	48	21	119	0	0	.266/.313/.449
2019	WAS	MLB	31	358	36	16	0	12	43	38	84	2	0	.223/.316/.389
2020	WAS	MLB	32	119	14	6	1	4	13	6	22	1	0	.284/.319/.468
2021 FS	WAS	MLB	33	600	69	27	1	20	75	38	157	1	1	.231/.293/.396
2021 DC	WAS	MLB	33	488	56	22	0	16	61	31	128	0	1	.231/.293/.396

Comparables: Adam Melhuse, Damian Miller, Welington Castillo

YEAR	TEAM	P. COUNT	FRM RUNS	BLK RUNS	THRW RUNS	TOT RUNS
2018	CLE	15311	7.5	1.7	0.0	9.3
2019	WAS	13282	-4.3	2.8	0.7	-0.9
2020	WAS	4477	-1.6	0.3	0.2	-1.1
2021	WAS	14430	-5.7	0.8	-0.4	-5.3
2021	WAS	14430	-5.7	1.8	-0.4	-4.3

For the last two seasons, Gomes has been half of Washington's solution to the loss of Wilson Ramos, pairing up with Kurt Suzuki to form a catcher tandem that was occasionally good and mostly adequate. At catcher, that's basically free real estate. Suzuki heading to free agency leaves Gomes atop the depth chart, but he shouldn't get cozy up there. Set to turn 34 in July and boasting a ceiling of "league average" at the plate and behind it, the Brazilian veteran is better suited staying in a part-time role or becoming the veteran backup to an up-and-coming youngster. The Nationals don't have one of those in stock, so until they do, expect Gomes to keep his part-time role alongside another older backstop looking for a place to crash for the next season or two. Yan's a pretty good roommate.

YEAR	TEAM	LVL	AGE	PA	DRC+	BABIP	BRR	FRAA	WARP
2018	CLE	MLB	30	435	102	.336	-1.1	C(111): 9.1	3.1
2019	WAS	MLB	31	358	91	.265	0.1	C(93): -1.6, 1B(1): -0.0	1.3
2020	WAS	MLB	32	119	108	.314	-0.5	C(30): 0.7	0.4
2021 FS	WAS	MLB	33	600	88	.285	-0.9	C -5, 1B 0	1.0
2021 DC	WAS	MLB	33	488	88	.285	-0.7	C -5, 1B 0	0.4

Yan Gomes, continued

Batted Ball Distribution

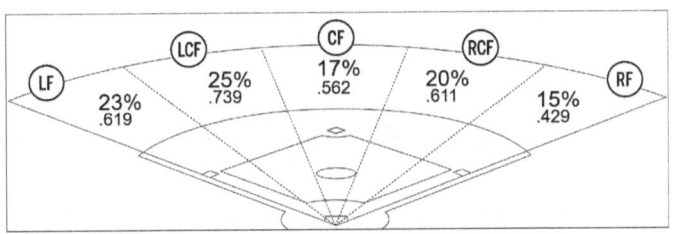

Strike Zone vs LHP   Strike Zone vs RHP

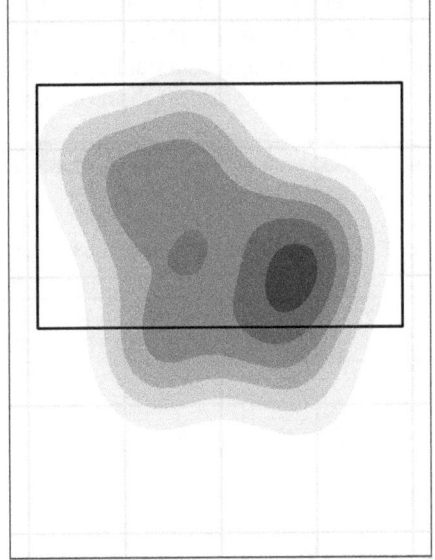

Washington Nationals 2021

Josh Harrison 2B
Born: 07/08/87 Age: 34 Bats: R Throws: R
Height: 5'8" Weight: 190 Origin: Round 6, 2008 Draft (#191 overall)

YEAR	TEAM	LVL	AGE	PA	R	2B	3B	HR	RBI	BB	K	SB	CS	AVG/OBP/SLG
2018	PIT	MLB	30	374	41	13	1	8	37	18	68	3	0	.250/.293/.363
2019	TOL	AAA	31	29	2	1	0	0	3	6	4	0	0	.174/.345/.217
2019	DET	MLB	31	147	10	7	1	1	8	6	27	4	2	.175/.218/.263
2020	WAS	MLB	32	91	11	2	0	3	14	6	12	1	2	.278/.352/.418
2021 FS	WAS	MLB	33	600	68	26	1	13	69	31	112	13	5	.247/.305/.378
2021 DC	WAS	MLB	33	237	27	10	0	5	27	12	44	5	2	.247/.305/.378

Comparables: Omar Infante, Adam Kennedy, Brandon Phillips

It's been a long time since Harrison was anything more than a likable yet below-average player, and a rough final season in Pittsburgh in 2018 plus a short and ugly stint with Detroit in '19 suggested that even those days were dead and gone. But like a phoenix rising from Arizona, he popped up on Washington's roster as part of a rotating infield carousel and posted a career-high on-base percentage and his best DRC+ figure since 2014. More walks, fewer strikeouts and better performance against fastballs (a .371 batting average and .657 slugging percentage) were the keys to his resurgence and earned him a one-year deal to stick around as a backup. The fun times likely won't last, but at least he's getting a happier sendoff than before.

YEAR	TEAM	LVL	AGE	PA	DRC+	BABIP	BRR	FRAA	WARP
2018	PIT	MLB	30	374	87	.286	0.5	2B(87): -5.6, 3B(2): -0.0	0.0
2019	TOL	AAA	31	29	105	.211	-0.9	2B(4): -0.1	0.0
2019	DET	MLB	31	147	63	.207	-1.1	2B(34): 2.7	-0.1
2020	WAS	MLB	32	91	118	.288	-0.4	2B(12): -0.5, 3B(10): -0.7, LF(5): 0.7	0.3
2021 FS	WAS	MLB	33	600	88	.288	0.5	3B -4, 1B 0	0.5
2021 DC	WAS	MLB	33	237	88	.288	0.2	3B -2, 1B 0	0.0

Josh Harrison, continued

Batted Ball Distribution

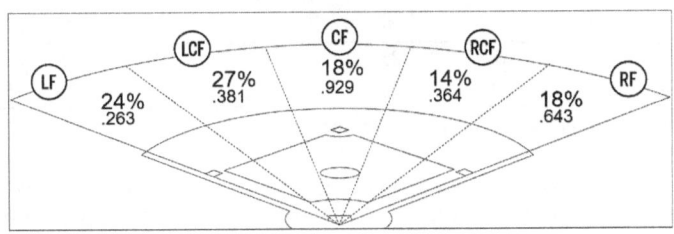

Strike Zone vs LHP   **Strike Zone vs RHP**

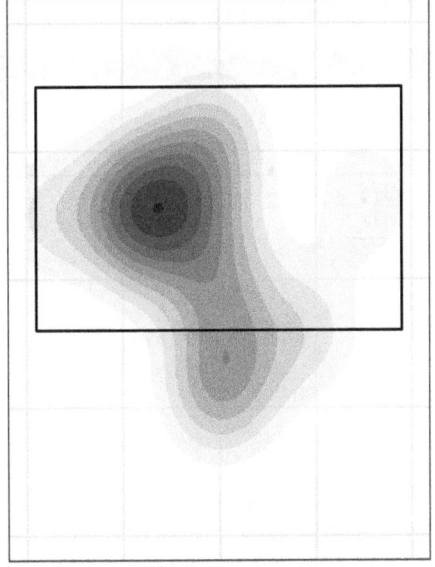

Howie Kendrick 2B

Born: 07/12/83 Age: 37 Bats: R Throws: R
Height: 5'11" Weight: 225 Origin: Round 10, 2002 Draft (#294 overall)

YEAR	TEAM	LVL	AGE	PA	R	2B	3B	HR	RBI	BB	K	SB	CS	AVG/OBP/SLG
2018	WAS	MLB	34	160	17	14	0	4	12	5	29	1	1	.303/.331/.474
2019	WAS	MLB	35	370	61	23	1	17	62	27	48	2	1	.344/.395/.572
2020	WAS	MLB	36	100	11	4	0	2	14	7	17	0	0	.275/.320/.385
2021 FS	*WAS*	*MLB*	*37*	*600*	*61*	*25*	*1*	*15*	*65*	*41*	*125*	*11*	*4*	*.259/.318/.395*
2021 DC	*WAS*	*MLB*	*37*	*300*	*30*	*12*	*0*	*7*	*32*	*20*	*62*	*5*	*2*	*.259/.318/.395*

Comparables: Brandon Phillips, Bret Boone, Randy Velarde

Sometimes, glory days, they pass you by. In Kendrick's case, they went by quickly. Less than a year after playing the hero throughout the Nationals' championship run—and then returning despite having a richer offer on the table from the Rays—he had one of the worst seasons of his career. Compared to 2019, he struck out more frequently and walked and made quality contact less frequently. Kendrick turned 37 in July, and while the normal sample-size caveats apply to his 2020, it's probably fair to say this professional hitter has seen his finest hours.

YEAR	TEAM	LVL	AGE	PA	DRC+	BABIP	BRR	FRAA	WARP
2018	WAS	MLB	34	160	94	.350	-3.1	2B(33): -2.7, LF(6): -0.1, 1B(2): 0.0	-0.2
2019	WAS	MLB	35	370	132	.358	-2.6	1B(48): 1.8, 2B(23): 0.7, 3B(15): -1.4	2.3
2020	WAS	MLB	36	100	93	.311	-0.3	1B(6): -0.0	0.0
2021 FS	*WAS*	*MLB*	*37*	*600*	*96*	*.310*	*0.1*	*2B -1, 1B 2*	*1.0*
2021 DC	*WAS*	*MLB*	*37*	*300*	*96*	*.310*	*0.1*	*2B -1, 1B 1*	*0.5*

Howie Kendrick, continued

Batted Ball Distribution

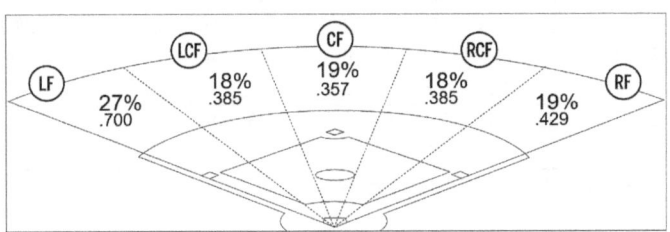

Strike Zone vs LHP   **Strike Zone vs RHP**

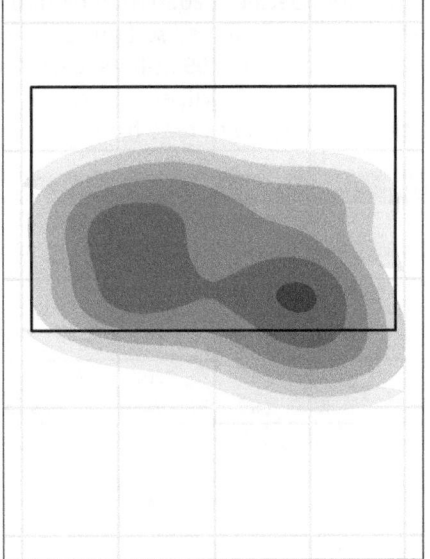

Carter Kieboom SS

Born: 09/03/97   Age: 23   Bats: R   Throws: R
Height: 6'2"   Weight: 210   Origin: Round 1, 2016 Draft (#28 overall)

YEAR	TEAM	LVL	AGE	PA	R	2B	3B	HR	RBI	BB	K	SB	CS	AVG/OBP/SLG
2018	FBG	HI-A	20	285	48	15	0	11	46	36	50	6	1	.298/.386/.494
2018	HBG	AA	20	273	36	16	1	5	23	22	59	3	1	.262/.326/.395
2019	FRE	AAA	21	494	79	24	3	16	79	68	100	5	2	.303/.409/.493
2019	WAS	MLB	21	43	4	0	0	2	2	4	16	0	0	.128/.209/.282
2020	WAS	MLB	22	122	15	1	0	0	9	17	33	0	1	.202/.344/.212
2021 FS	WAS	MLB	23	600	71	22	1	16	68	60	171	0	1	.223/.312/.368
2021 DC	WAS	MLB	23	443	52	16	1	12	50	44	126	0	1	.223/.312/.368

Comparables: B.J. Upton, Willy Adames, Corey Seager

Many of us learned how to bake bread during quarantine, and that means that we also learned that the loaf doesn't always turn out how you wanted it to—especially when you're a novice. Kieboom is starting to look like one of those March loaves. He's now more than 150 at-bats into his big-league career, and neither his bat nor his glove have proven worthy of his lofty prospect status. He did field better in 2020 than he had during his initial cup-of-coffee cameo in 2019, but his bat played so light as to be captured in a single statistic: he had one extra base hit in 99 at-bats. One. Another rotten year and it'll be time to wonder if Kieboom will ever rise, or if the Nationals should give up baking and stick to buying their bread from the store.

YEAR	TEAM	LVL	AGE	PA	DRC+	BABIP	BRR	FRAA	WARP
2018	FBG	HI-A	20	285	156	.332	0.5	SS(56): -0.4	2.3
2018	HBG	AA	20	273	106	.324	0.5	SS(62): 2.6	1.3
2019	FRE	AAA	21	494	126	.362	1.4	SS(62): -3.7, 2B(41): 3.2, 3B(10): -0.1	3.5
2019	WAS	MLB	21	43	61	.143	0.1	SS(10): -1.0	-0.1
2020	WAS	MLB	22	122	85	.299	1.4	3B(31): 3.7	0.5
2021 FS	WAS	MLB	23	600	89	.295	-0.8	3B 6, 2B 0	1.4
2021 DC	WAS	MLB	23	443	89	.295	-0.6	3B 4	0.6

Carter Kieboom, continued

Batted Ball Distribution

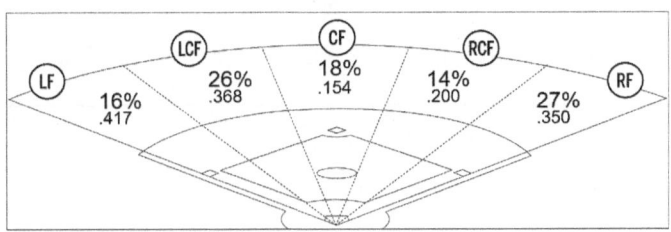

Strike Zone vs LHP   **Strike Zone vs RHP**

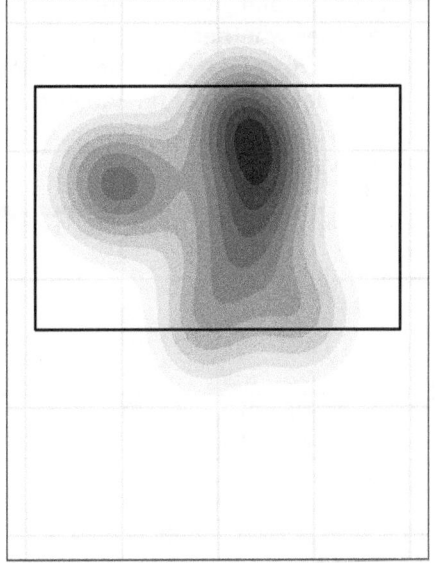

Victor Robles CF

Born: 05/19/97   Age: 24   Bats: R   Throws: R
Height: 6'0"   Weight: 205   Origin: International Free Agent, 2013

YEAR	TEAM	LVL	AGE	PA	R	2B	3B	HR	RBI	BB	K	SB	CS	AVG/OBP/SLG
2018	NAT	ROK	21	27	7	1	0	0	1	7	4	4	1	.333/.556/.389
2018	SYR	AAA	21	182	25	9	1	2	10	18	26	14	6	.278/.356/.386
2018	WAS	MLB	21	66	8	3	1	3	10	4	12	3	2	.288/.348/.525
2019	WAS	MLB	22	617	86	33	3	17	65	35	140	28	9	.255/.326/.419
2020	WAS	MLB	23	189	20	5	1	3	15	9	53	4	1	.220/.293/.315
2021 FS	WAS	MLB	24	600	76	22	3	16	67	39	152	22	10	.232/.315/.381
2021 DC	WAS	MLB	24	515	65	19	3	14	57	33	130	19	8	.232/.315/.381

Comparables: Dale Murphy, Chris Young, Adam Jones

Poor Robles, who went from crown prince in D.C. as the top prospect and heir apparent to Bryce Harper in the outfield to having Juan Soto steal every last ounce of his thunder. Not that he's earning himself any spotlights after cratering offensively in 2020, when a total lack of plate discipline and power combined to make him Jeff Mathis But Fast. The good news is there's nowhere to go from there but up, and given that he's still just 24 with loud tools, the Nationals can wait and see whether he can climb out of his hole. If nothing else, he's still a great defender and baserunner. It's adjusting to major-league pitching that's been the hardest part, and Robles hasn't shown any consistent signs of figuring things out; if anything, he's going backwards. Heavy is the head that wears the crown, even briefly.

YEAR	TEAM	LVL	AGE	PA	DRC+	BABIP	BRR	FRAA	WARP
2018	NAT	ROK	21	27		.429			
2018	SYR	AAA	21	182	100	.318	1.2	CF(39): -0.8	0.4
2018	WAS	MLB	21	66	103	.311	0.7	CF(14): 0.1, LF(2): 0.0, RF(2): -0.2	0.3
2019	WAS	MLB	22	617	84	.310	5.6	CF(141): 6.6, RF(15): 1.1	2.3
2020	WAS	MLB	23	189	72	.298	2.8	CF(52): 0.4	0.2
2021 FS	WAS	MLB	24	600	93	.293	2.0	CF 5, LF 0	2.2
2021 DC	WAS	MLB	24	515	93	.293	1.7	CF 5	1.9

Victor Robles, continued

Batted Ball Distribution

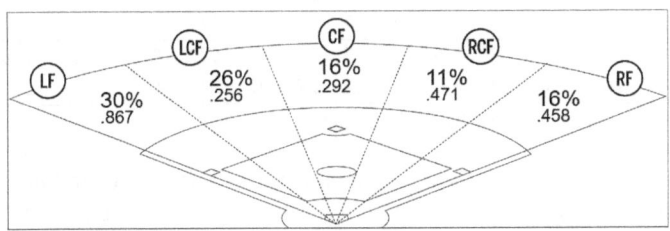

Strike Zone vs LHP **Strike Zone vs RHP**

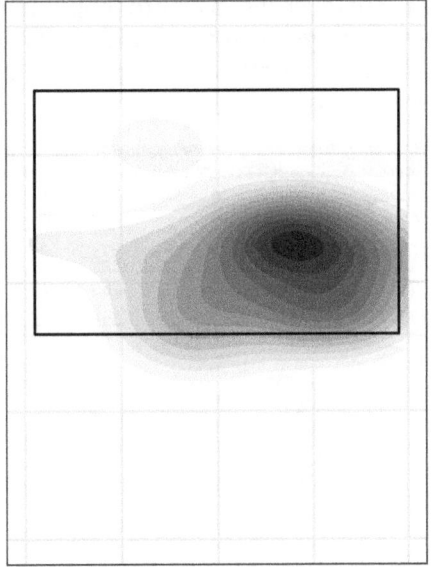

Kyle Schwarber LF

Born: 03/05/93 Age: 28 Bats: L Throws: R
Height: 6'0" Weight: 225 Origin: Round 1, 2014 Draft (#4 overall)

YEAR	TEAM	LVL	AGE	PA	R	2B	3B	HR	RBI	BB	K	SB	CS	AVG/OBP/SLG
2018	CHC	MLB	25	510	64	14	3	26	61	78	140	4	3	.238/.356/.467
2019	CHC	MLB	26	610	82	29	3	38	92	70	156	2	3	.250/.339/.531
2020	CHC	MLB	27	224	30	6	0	11	24	30	66	1	0	.188/.308/.393
2021 FS	WAS	MLB	28	600	89	23	2	31	87	83	180	3	2	.230/.344/.470
2021 DC	WAS	MLB	28	560	83	21	2	29	81	77	168	3	2	.230/.344/.470

Comparables: Jonny Gomes, Jason Michaels, Pat Burrell

The key to Schwarber's success is simple: hit the ball hard, hit the ball high and let physics do its thing. He used that philosophy to good effect during his career-year in 2019, and it seemed to carry over to the start of 2020. Through the end of August, he was hitting a Schwarberian .228/.333/.500 with nine home runs. But while Schwarber was hitting the ball hard, he wasn't hitting it all that high. A career-worst launch angle precipitated a September that probably left him humming a certain Green Day song while in the batter's box. Maybe it's unfair to read too much into a month-long slump during a shortened season, but it felt like the progress he had made came undone. Schwarber is now entering his walk year, and if there's one piece of advice we'd give him, it's this: lift and separate.

YEAR	TEAM	LVL	AGE	PA	DRC+	BABIP	BRR	FRAA	WARP
2018	CHC	MLB	25	510	111	.288	-3.4	LF(120): 2.7	1.9
2019	CHC	MLB	26	610	120	.276	-5.0	LF(140): -0.6, C(1): 0.1	2.7
2020	CHC	MLB	27	224	96	.219	-0.8	LF(48): -0.5	0.3
2021 FS	WAS	MLB	28	600	122	.288	-0.4	LF 2, C 0	3.4
2021 DC	WAS	MLB	28	560	122	.288	-0.4	LF 2	3.0

Kyle Schwarber, continued

Batted Ball Distribution

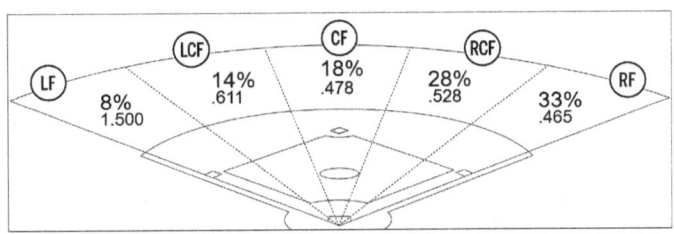

Strike Zone vs LHP   **Strike Zone vs RHP**

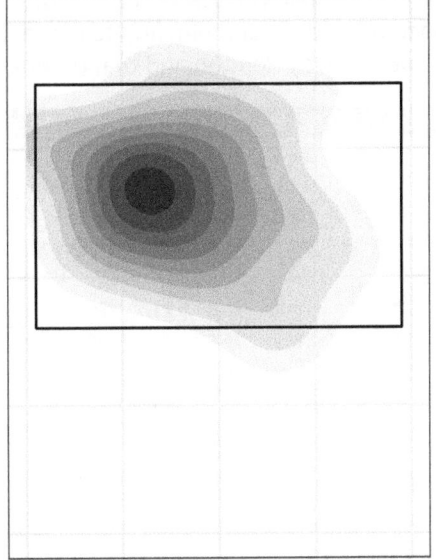

Washington Nationals 2021

Juan Soto LF

Born: 10/25/98   Age: 22   Bats: L   Throws: L
Height: 6'1"   Weight: 220   Origin: International Free Agent, 2015

YEAR	TEAM	LVL	AGE	PA	R	2B	3B	HR	RBI	BB	K	SB	CS	AVG/OBP/SLG
2018	HAG	LO-A	19	74	12	5	3	5	24	14	13	2	0	.373/.486/.814
2018	FBG	HI-A	19	73	17	3	1	7	18	11	8	0	1	.371/.466/.790
2018	HBG	AA	19	35	4	2	0	2	10	4	7	1	0	.323/.400/.581
2018	WAS	MLB	19	494	77	25	1	22	70	79	99	5	2	.292/.406/.517
2019	WAS	MLB	20	659	110	32	5	34	110	108	132	12	1	.282/.401/.548
2020	WAS	MLB	21	196	39	14	0	13	37	41	28	6	2	.351/.490/.695
2021 FS	WAS	MLB	22	600	101	29	3	29	94	99	109	6	3	.294/.414/.539
2021 DC	WAS	MLB	22	641	108	31	3	30	101	106	116	7	3	.294/.414/.539

Comparables: Adam Dunn, Carlos May, Curt Blefary

Soto continued to do Soto things: hit, hit for power, take his walks and even field a competent left field. Despite Soto's narrative parallels with a certain other highly touted former Nationals outfielder, he's closer to Anthony Rendon as a player. He walks far more than he strikes out, he chases little and wastes rarely and he smiles with his teeth. The Nationals found a diamond: the challenge now is to rebuild around him and to not let him walk out the door in a few years' time, the way Rendon and that other guy have the past couple winters.

YEAR	TEAM	LVL	AGE	PA	DRC+	BABIP	BRR	FRAA	WARP
2018	HAG	LO-A	19	74	214	.405	0.3	RF(14): 1.1, CF(2): 0.2	1.1
2018	FBG	HI-A	19	73	250	.340	1.4	RF(14): 1.0, LF(1): 0.0	1.4
2018	HBG	AA	19	35	113	.364	0.0	LF(4): 0.6, RF(4): -0.5	0.1
2018	WAS	MLB	19	494	125	.338	-0.5	LF(114): 2.7	3.0
2019	WAS	MLB	20	659	135	.312	1.4	LF(150): -0.8	4.9
2020	WAS	MLB	21	196	170	.363	-1.0	LF(36): -2.8, RF(6): -0.6	1.6
2021 FS	WAS	MLB	22	600	160	.327	-0.1	RF 2, LF 0	6.4
2021 DC	WAS	MLB	22	641	160	.327	-0.1	RF 2, LF 0	6.5

Juan Soto, continued

Batted Ball Distribution

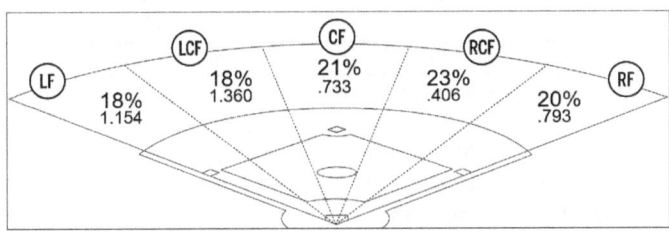

Strike Zone vs LHP   **Strike Zone vs RHP**

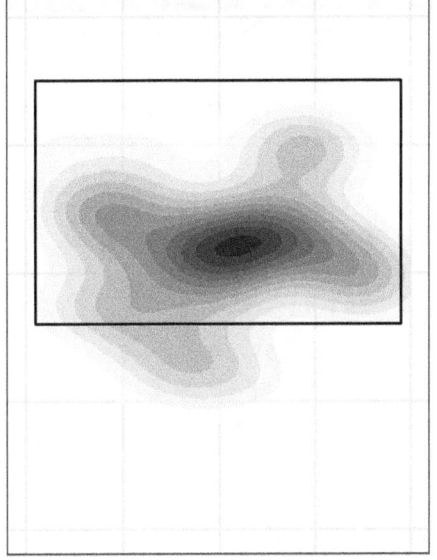

Washington Nationals 2021

Eric Thames 1B
Born: 11/10/86   Age: 34   Bats: L   Throws: R
Height: 5'11"   Weight: 235   Origin: Round 7, 2008 Draft (#219 overall)

YEAR	TEAM	LVL	AGE	PA	R	2B	3B	HR	RBI	BB	K	SB	CS	AVG/OBP/SLG
2018	MIL	MLB	31	278	41	10	3	16	37	29	97	7	0	.219/.306/.478
2019	MIL	MLB	32	459	67	23	2	25	61	51	140	3	2	.247/.346/.505
2020	WAS	MLB	33	140	10	5	0	3	12	14	42	1	0	.203/.300/.317
2021 FS	WAS	MLB	34	600	69	23	2	24	75	67	196	6	3	.214/.315/.406

Comparables: Brandon Moss, Dave Kingman, Carlos Pena

The Nationals signed Thames to mash against righties—he had slugged better than .500 against them in 2019—as part of a first-base platoon with Ryan Zimmerman. By the time the season started, Zimmerman had opted out over COVID-related concerns. Thames' bat did the same, leaving the Nationals with a colder-than-usual cold corner. He'll spend 2021 in Tokyo as a member of the Yomiuri Giants, hoping that another tour of Asia can defibrillate his career a second time.

YEAR	TEAM	LVL	AGE	PA	DRC+	BABIP	BRR	FRAA	WARP
2018	MIL	MLB	31	278	96	.284	2.3	RF(31): -0.3, 1B(29): -0.9, LF(10): 0.7	0.6
2019	MIL	MLB	32	459	111	.313	1.8	1B(105): -1.4, RF(12): -0.1	1.5
2020	WAS	MLB	33	140	80	.282	-0.6	1B(27): 0.1	-0.1
2021 FS	WAS	MLB	34	600	97	.292	0.0	1B 1, RF 0	0.8

Eric Thames, continued

Batted Ball Distribution

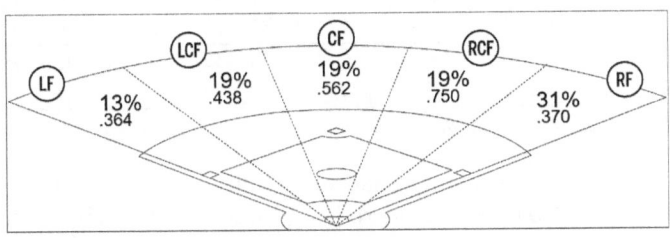

Strike Zone vs LHP   **Strike Zone vs RHP**

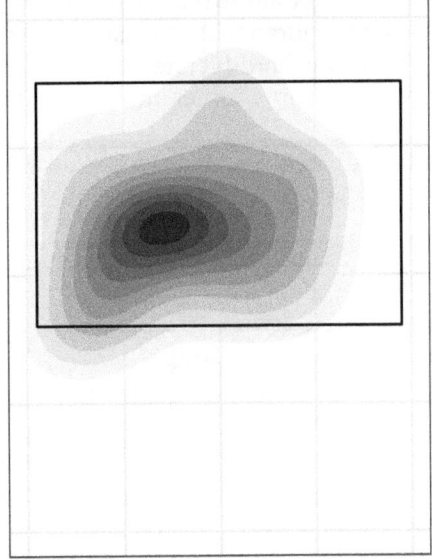

Washington Nationals 2021

Trea Turner SS

Born: 06/30/93   Age: 28   Bats: R   Throws: R
Height: 6'2"   Weight: 185   Origin: Round 1, 2014 Draft (#13 overall)

YEAR	TEAM	LVL	AGE	PA	R	2B	3B	HR	RBI	BB	K	SB	CS	AVG/OBP/SLG
2018	WAS	MLB	25	740	103	27	6	19	73	69	132	43	9	.271/.344/.416
2019	WAS	MLB	26	569	96	37	5	19	57	43	113	35	5	.298/.353/.497
2020	WAS	MLB	27	259	46	15	4	12	41	22	36	12	4	.335/.394/.588
2021 FS	WAS	MLB	28	600	94	30	5	21	74	50	110	36	10	.291/.354/.485
2021 DC	WAS	MLB	28	670	105	33	5	23	83	55	123	40	11	.291/.354/.485

Comparables: Brad Miller, Stephen Drew, Derek Jeter

Those middling two seasons that had some folks questioning Turner's 2016 breakout are starting to look less like red flags and more like a hyper-talented young hitter figuring things out. He put together his best year since that aforementioned 73-game '16 campaign, posting a career-high DRC+ and leading the majors in hits, to make it two straight seasons of above-average offense. Even better, this one was fueled by fewer strikeouts, fewer swings and misses—particularly on the breaking balls that had been eating him alive—and more walks than 2019; he went from 91st in strikeout percentage to 22nd. That's the kind of jump that you just love to see, and coupled with an uptick in exit velocity and hard-hit rate that's stuck, plus his Olympic-caliber speed and good defense, it turns Turner into a dark horse NL MVP pick for 2021.

YEAR	TEAM	LVL	AGE	PA	DRC+	BABIP	BRR	FRAA	WARP
2018	WAS	MLB	25	740	106	.314	2.7	SS(159): 7.1	5.0
2019	WAS	MLB	26	569	107	.348	4.1	SS(122): 3.8	4.0
2020	WAS	MLB	27	259	137	.353	5.0	SS(59): -7.8	1.5
2021 FS	WAS	MLB	28	600	130	.331	2.9	SS 1	4.5
2021 DC	WAS	MLB	28	670	130	.331	3.3	SS 1	5.0

Trea Turner, continued

Batted Ball Distribution

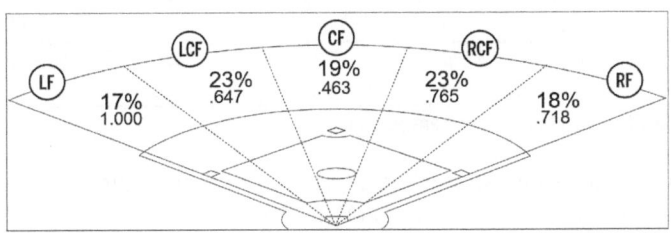

Strike Zone vs LHP   **Strike Zone vs RHP**

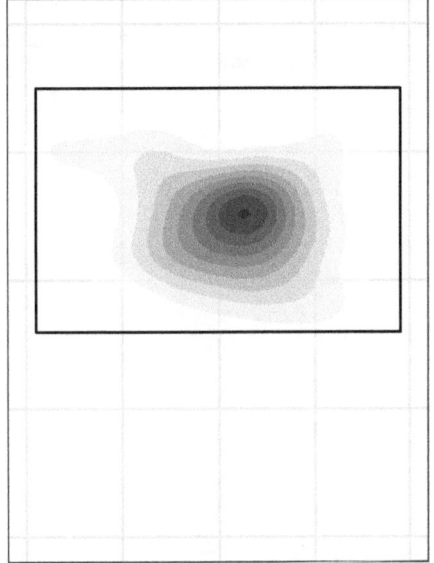

Dakota Bacus   RHP

Born: 04/02/91   Age: 30   Bats: R   Throws: R
Height: 6'2"   Weight: 220   Origin: Round 9, 2012 Draft (#289 overall)

YEAR	TEAM	LVL	AGE	W	L	SV	G	GS	IP	H	HR	BB/9	K/9	K	GB%	BABIP
2018	HBG	AA	27	2	1	2	26	0	37	36	1	3.2	11.7	48	53.7%	.372
2019	FRE	AAA	28	5	5	9	46	0	55^1	50	3	4.6	8.5	52	40.4%	.301
2020	WAS	MLB	29	0	0	0	11	0	11^1	14	1	7.1	5.6	7	46.3%	.325
2021 FS	*WAS*	*MLB*	*30*	*2*	*3*	*0*	*57*	*0*	*50*	*48*	*7*	*4.6*	*8.0*	*44*	*43.5%*	*.289*
2021 DC	*WAS*	*MLB*	*30*	*2*	*2*	*0*	*48*	*0*	*40.7*	*39*	*6*	*4.6*	*8.0*	*36*	*43.5%*	*.289*

Comparables: Jacob Barnes, Cole Sulser, Sam Selman

Bacus' name makes him sound like a tertiary Kurt Vonnegut character, a four-year starting linebacker on a mid-tier MAC football team or a grizzled rodeo champion. No one's going to mistake him for a major league-caliber reliever after the year he had.

YEAR	TEAM	LVL	AGE	WHIP	ERA	DRA-	WARP	MPH	FB%	WHF	CSP
2018	HBG	AA	27	1.32	3.89	50	1.1				
2019	FRE	AAA	28	1.41	3.58	70	1.5				
2020	WAS	MLB	29	2.03	7.94	120	0.0	92.3	34.2%	24.0%	
2021 FS	*WAS*	*MLB*	*30*	*1.48*	*4.87*	*107*	*0.0*	*92.3*	*34.2%*	*24.0%*	*46.1%*
2021 DC	*WAS*	*MLB*	*30*	*1.48*	*4.87*	*107*	*0.0*	*92.3*	*34.2%*	*24.0%*	*46.1%*

Dakota Bacus, continued

Pitch Shape vs LHH

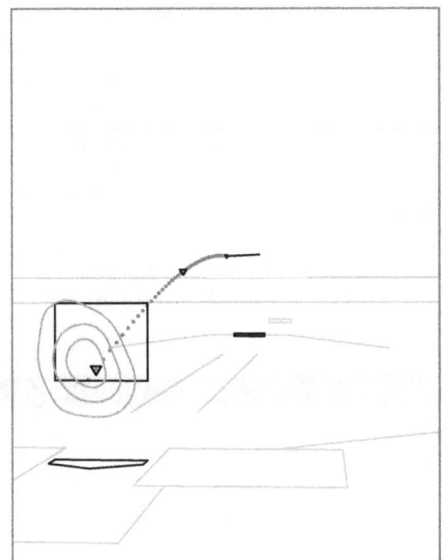

Pitch Shape vs RHH

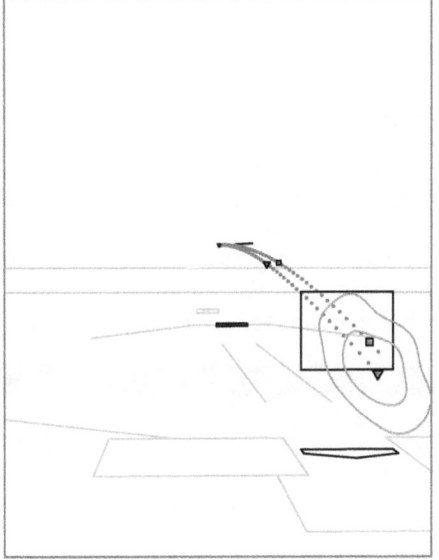

Type	Frequency	Velocity	H Movement	V Movement
☐ Sinker	33.8%	90.9 [92]	-10.5 [119]	-25.3 [84]
▽ Slider	60.4%	85.4 [106]	2.9 [91]	-32.1 [105]
◇ Curveball	5.3%	77.7 [96]	11.3 [115]	-51.7 [93]

Washington Nationals 2021

Ben Braymer LHP
Born: 04/28/94 Age: 27 Bats: L Throws: L
Height: 6'2" Weight: 220 Origin: Round 18, 2016 Draft (#544 overall)

YEAR	TEAM	LVL	AGE	W	L	SV	G	GS	IP	H	HR	BB/9	K/9	K	GB%	BABIP
2018	HAG	LO-A	24	3	0	0	7	0	25^2	18	2	1.8	8.8	25	50.8%	.262
2018	FBG	HI-A	24	6	3	2	21	11	89	73	4	2.9	9.4	93	38.0%	.296
2019	HBG	AA	25	4	4	0	13	13	79	56	7	2.4	7.9	69	31.1%	.228
2019	FRE	AAA	25	0	6	0	13	13	60	81	18	5.2	7.0	47	33.0%	.346
2020	WAS	MLB	26	1	0	0	3	1	7^1	7	0	6.1	9.8	8	28.6%	.333
2021 FS	*WAS*	*MLB*	*27*	*2*	*3*	*0*	*57*	*0*	*50*	*53*	*10*	*4.2*	*8.1*	*45*	*32.8%*	*.301*
2021 DC	*WAS*	*MLB*	*27*	*4*	*3*	*0*	*42*	*3*	*43*	*45*	*8*	*4.2*	*8.1*	*38*	*32.8%*	*.301*

Comparables: Caleb Baragar, Dillon Maples, Locke St. John

Despite being a soft-tossing lefty, Braymer racked up a fair number of strikeouts and also handed out far too many walks, defying all our beliefs of what it means to be a crafty southpaw.

YEAR	TEAM	LVL	AGE	WHIP	ERA	DRA-	WARP	MPH	FB%	WHF	CSP
2018	HAG	LO-A	24	0.90	1.75	76	0.4				
2018	FBG	HI-A	24	1.15	2.43	81	1.5				
2019	HBG	AA	25	0.97	2.51	67	1.6				
2019	FRE	AAA	25	1.93	7.20	189	-1.4				
2020	WAS	MLB	26	1.64	1.23	113	0.0	90.1	53.9%	20.7%	
2021 FS	*WAS*	*MLB*	*27*	*1.53*	*5.67*	*122*	*-0.4*	*90.1*	*53.9%*	*20.7%*	*40.2%*
2021 DC	*WAS*	*MLB*	*27*	*1.53*	*5.67*	*122*	*-0.2*	*90.1*	*53.9%*	*20.7%*	*40.2%*

Ben Braymer, continued

Pitch Shape vs LHH	Pitch Shape vs RHH
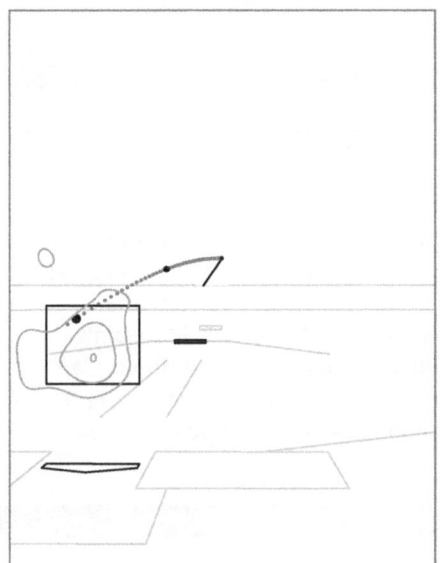	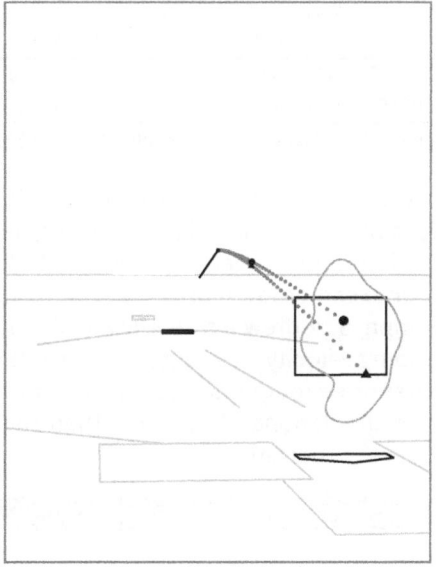

Type	Frequency	Velocity	H Movement	V Movement
● Fastball	53.9%	88.9 [88]	9.1 [88]	-15.8 [98]
▲ Changeup	22.4%	79.2 [77]	10.8 [105]	-29 [96]
◇ Curveball	23.7%	76.5 [92]	-3 [81]	-49.2 [98]

Patrick Corbin LHP

Born: 07/19/89   Age: 31   Bats: L   Throws: L
Height: 6'3"   Weight: 210   Origin: Round 2, 2009 Draft (#80 overall)

YEAR	TEAM	LVL	AGE	W	L	SV	G	GS	IP	H	HR	BB/9	K/9	K	GB%	BABIP
2018	ARI	MLB	28	11	7	0	33	33	200	162	15	2.2	11.1	246	48.5%	.304
2019	WAS	MLB	29	14	7	0	33	33	202	169	24	3.1	10.6	238	48.7%	.295
2020	WAS	MLB	30	2	7	0	11	11	65^2	85	10	2.5	8.2	60	45.2%	.362
2021 FS	WAS	MLB	31	9	8	0	26	26	150	143	20	3.0	9.1	151	47.0%	.299
2021 DC	WAS	MLB	31	11	9	0	29	29	169	161	23	3.0	9.1	170	47.0%	.299

Comparables: Jake Odorizzi, Sonny Gray, Nathan Eovaldi

There is something up—or, rather, down—with Corbin's fastball velocity. Corbin's never been a flamethrower; he's instead relied on his devastating slider and how it plays off his low-90s heat. His velocity dipped a full two miles per hour to career-low marks in 2020. His slider's efficacy went down with his oomph, as it drew a career-low whiff rate. It remains to be seen if Corbin's dipping velocity was caused by the unusual season, aging, conditioning, an unreported (or undiagnosed) injury or some combination thereof. Whatever the case, the Nationals have more than 106 million reasons to hope that it was a one-year aberration.

YEAR	TEAM	LVL	AGE	WHIP	ERA	DRA-	WARP	MPH	FB%	WHF	CSP
2018	ARI	MLB	28	1.05	3.15	61	5.9	93.4	48.6%	34.7%	
2019	WAS	MLB	29	1.18	3.25	63	5.9	94.0	53.6%	31.8%	
2020	WAS	MLB	30	1.57	4.66	98	0.6	92.3	52.2%	23.7%	
2021 FS	WAS	MLB	31	1.29	3.94	91	2.1	93.5	52.0%	30.5%	43.3%
2021 DC	WAS	MLB	31	1.29	3.94	91	2.4	93.5	52.0%	30.5%	43.3%

Patrick Corbin, continued

Pitch Shape vs LHH

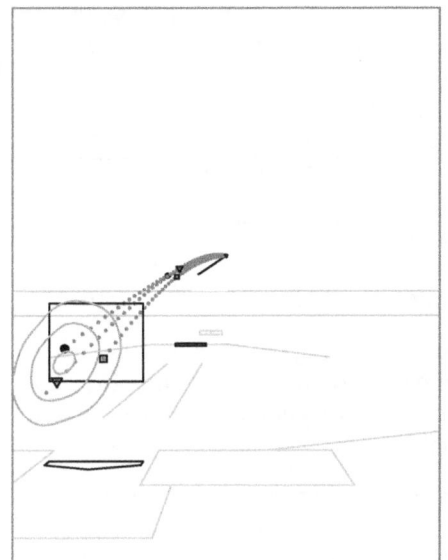

Pitch Shape vs RHH

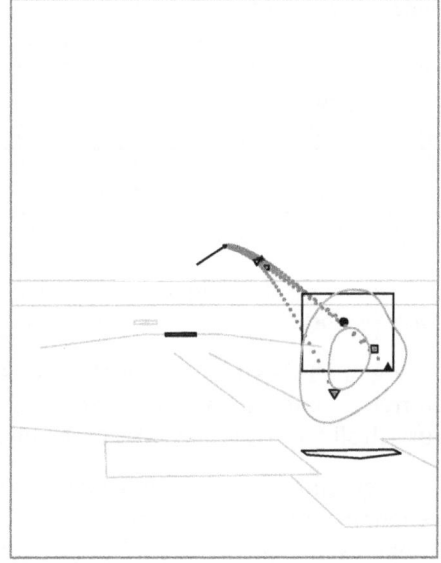

Type	Frequency	Velocity	H Movement	V Movement
● Fastball	20.4%	90.4 [93]	7.5 [96]	-16.5 [96]
☐ Sinker	31.5%	90.3 [89]	12.2 [106]	-19.3 [104]
▲ Changeup	5.6%	77.8 [71]	9.4 [112]	-30.6 [92]
▽ Slider	40.0%	79.4 [80]	-3.3 [93]	-38.3 [87]

Washington Nationals 2021

Erick Fedde RHP
Born: 02/25/93 Age: 28 Bats: R Throws: R
Height: 6'4" Weight: 200 Origin: Round 1, 2014 Draft (#18 overall)

YEAR	TEAM	LVL	AGE	W	L	SV	G	GS	IP	H	HR	BB/9	K/9	K	GB%	BABIP
2018	SYR	AAA	25	3	3	0	13	13	67.1	78	3	2.4	9.4	70	48.7%	.393
2018	WAS	MLB	25	2	4	0	11	11	50.1	55	8	3.9	8.2	46	53.0%	.336
2019	HBG	AA	26	2	0	0	5	4	24.2	18	2	1.8	9.9	27	50.8%	.262
2019	FRE	AAA	26	1	1	0	2	2	10	19	5	3.6	9.0	10	36.1%	.452
2019	WAS	MLB	26	4	2	0	21	12	78	81	11	3.8	4.7	41	48.8%	.288
2020	WAS	MLB	27	2	4	0	11	8	50.1	47	10	3.9	5.0	28	55.0%	.234
2021 FS	WAS	MLB	28	9	9	0	26	26	150	152	22	3.5	6.9	114	51.9%	.288
2021 DC	WAS	MLB	28	3	3	0	16	11	47.3	48	7	3.5	6.9	36	51.9%	.288

Comparables: Daniel Mengden, Jeff Hoffman, Luis Perdomo

Fedde. /FEH-dee/. Noun. A bendy pitch not otherwise categorized as a slider, curve or slurve.

Origin: The "Fedde" as a pitch type came into common usage circa 2019-20, with Nationals pitcher Erick Fedde, who began classifying his sliderish curve (or curvish slider) as, simply, his "breaking ball."

Usage: Opponents either feasted or starved against the Fedde in 2019-20, depending on how it's classified. If combined into a single pitch, the Fedde was its namesake's most effective pitch over the two-year period. If separated, the more slider-ish Fedde held opponents to a sub-.200 batting average against, as opposed to the .341 average they posted against the more curve-ish variety.

Alternative usage: If a certain pitcher wants to stick on a big-league staff heading forward, then he should consider mastering throwing the sharper Fedde more frequently.

YEAR	TEAM	LVL	AGE	WHIP	ERA	DRA-	WARP	MPH	FB%	WHF	CSP
2018	SYR	AAA	25	1.43	4.41	83	1.1				
2018	WAS	MLB	25	1.53	5.54	108	0.3	95.9	54.9%	23.3%	
2019	HBG	AA	26	0.93	2.55	64	0.5				
2019	FRE	AAA	26	2.30	12.60	185	-0.2				
2019	WAS	MLB	26	1.46	4.50	128	-0.5	94.3	55.2%	16.8%	
2020	WAS	MLB	27	1.37	4.29	118	0.0	95.0	55.5%	15.3%	
2021 FS	WAS	MLB	28	1.40	4.63	104	1.1	94.8	55.3%	17.2%	45.9%
2021 DC	WAS	MLB	28	1.40	4.63	104	0.3	94.8	55.3%	17.2%	45.9%

Erick Fedde, continued

Pitch Shape vs LHH	Pitch Shape vs RHH
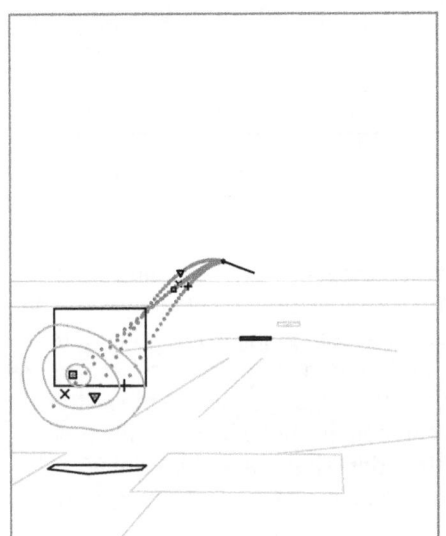	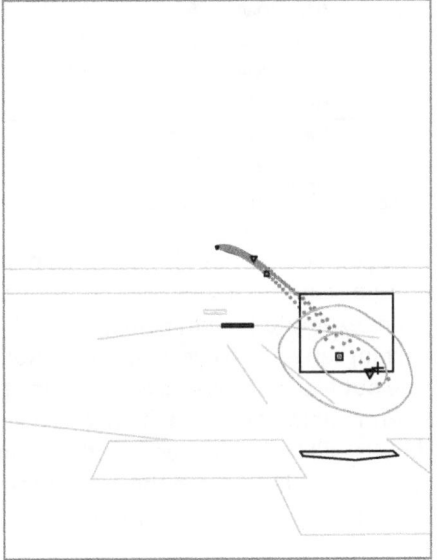

Type	Frequency	Velocity	H Movement	V Movement
☐ Sinker	55.1%	93.6 [106]	-8.3 [135]	-19.9 [102]
+ Cutter	16.4%	88.9 [103]	3.6 [111]	-25.9 [93]
✕ Splitter	9.4%	86.8 [107]	-11.8 [85]	-32.3 [90]
▽ Slider	16.8%	79.8 [82]	11.1 [122]	-39.7 [83]

Washington Nationals 2021

Kyle Finnegan   RHP
Born: 09/04/91   Age: 29   Bats: R   Throws: R
Height: 6'2"   Weight: 200   Origin: Round 6, 2013 Draft (#191 overall)

YEAR	TEAM	LVL	AGE	W	L	SV	G	GS	IP	H	HR	BB/9	K/9	K	GB%	BABIP
2018	MID	AA	26	1	1	13	21	0	25	18	0	4.0	10.1	28	62.5%	.286
2018	NAS	AAA	26	0	2	1	13	0	17²	22	2	3.6	8.7	17	39.7%	.357
2019	MID	AA	27	0	1	9	21	0	22²	16	0	2.8	14.3	36	54.2%	.333
2019	LV	AAA	27	3	1	5	21	0	28	23	3	3.9	11.6	36	40.9%	.323
2020	WAS	MLB	28	1	0	0	25	0	24²	21	2	4.7	9.5	26	50.0%	.292
2021 FS	WAS	MLB	29	2	2	0	57	0	50	43	5	4.8	10.1	56	47.9%	.295
2021 DC	WAS	MLB	29	2	2	0	54	0	52.3	45	5	4.8	10.1	58	47.9%	.295

Comparables: Eric Yardley, Brandon Brennan, Phillips Valdez

Do you ever wonder if the A's get mad when they let a player go and watch another team steal their bit of turning trash into treasure? Max Muncy is the best recent example of that; Finnegan might be the latest, going from Oakland to Washington after six years in the minors and emerging as a useful relief arm. He gave out too many walks to climb any higher than "guy you use in the sixth or seventh inning and not with a lead if you can help it," but a 95 mph sinker will play, as will the 50 percent whiff rate on his slider. That makes him a nice candidate to hold down the middle innings going forward—and if he can trim the walks, maybe he can graduate to bigger responsibilities.

YEAR	TEAM	LVL	AGE	WHIP	ERA	DRA-	WARP	MPH	FB%	WHF	CSP
2018	MID	AA	26	1.16	2.16	66	0.5				
2018	NAS	AAA	26	1.64	7.13	80	0.3				
2019	MID	AA	27	1.01	1.59	51	0.6				
2019	LV	AAA	27	1.25	2.89	50	1.0				
2020	WAS	MLB	28	1.38	2.92	85	0.4	96.6	70.4%	28.3%	
2021 FS	WAS	MLB	29	1.40	4.02	91	0.5	96.6	70.4%	28.3%	51.1%
2021 DC	WAS	MLB	29	1.40	4.02	91	0.5	96.6	70.4%	28.3%	51.1%

Kyle Finnegan, continued

Pitch Shape vs LHH

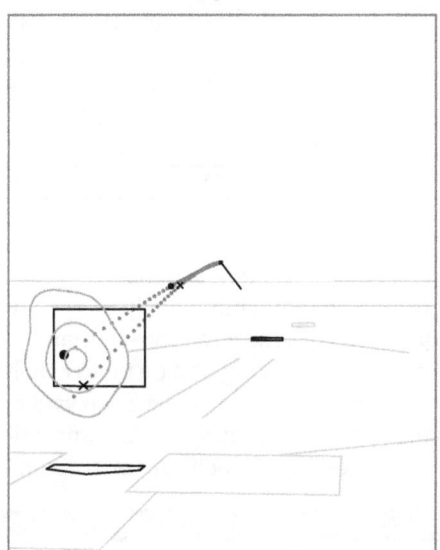

Pitch Shape vs RHH

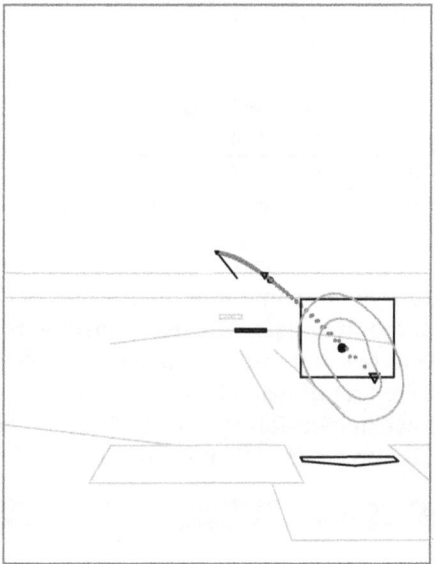

Type	Frequency	Velocity	H Movement	V Movement
● Fastball	67.8%	95.2 [108]	-9.2 [88]	-13.5 [105]
✕ Splitter	9.2%	87.1 [109]	-5.7 [108]	-26.8 [108]
▽ Slider	19.3%	87.4 [115]	4.6 [97]	-26.4 [121]

Washington Nationals 2021

Javy Guerra   RHP
Born: 10/31/85   Age: 35   Bats: R   Throws: R
Height: 6'1"   Weight: 216   Origin: Round 4, 2004 Draft (#118 overall)

YEAR	TEAM	LVL	AGE	W	L	SV	G	GS	IP	H	HR	BB/9	K/9	K	GB%	BABIP
2018	NO	AAA	32	3	0	5	12	0	16^2	9	0	1.6	13.0	24	57.6%	.281
2018	MIA	MLB	32	1	1	1	32	0	35^2	42	4	3.0	7.6	30	43.6%	.342
2019	BUF	AAA	33	0	1	1	5	0	7^1	4	0	4.9	7.4	6	27.8%	.222
2019	WAS	MLB	33	3	1	1	40	0	53^2	55	9	2.0	7.0	42	33.9%	.279
2019	TOR	MLB	33	0	0	1	11	0	14	12	1	3.2	9.6	15	26.3%	.306
2020	WAS	MLB	34	0	0	0	14	0	15^2	19	2	4.0	7.5	13	28.0%	.354
2021 FS	WAS	MLB	35	2	2	0	57	0	50	50	8	3.1	7.5	41	36.1%	.286

Comparables: Joe Smith, Jared Hughes, John Wyatt

Guerra's name means war, but his presence in a game tends to mean surrender—sometimes on the part of the opposing team, but usually on the part of the Nationals, who used him over the past two seasons as a mop-up man. Guerra's real value has been in an off-the-field role, working as a de facto coach to the refurbished Nationals bullpen. Considering his insights have been said to have helped Tanner Rainey throw strikes more frequently, maybe his name will take on a different meaning heading forward—like, say, "coach" or "instructor."

YEAR	TEAM	LVL	AGE	WHIP	ERA	DRA-	WARP	MPH	FB%	WHF	CSP
2018	NO	AAA	32	0.72	0.00	45	0.6				
2018	MIA	MLB	32	1.51	5.55	112	0.0	95.2	52.2%	19.5%	
2019	BUF	AAA	33	1.09	2.45	101	0.1				
2019	WAS	MLB	33	1.25	4.86	96	0.3	95.2	60.0%	19.1%	
2019	TOR	MLB	33	1.21	3.86	142	-0.2	95.4	56.1%	17.2%	
2020	WAS	MLB	34	1.66	4.02	121	0.0	93.7	67.0%	25.0%	
2021 FS	WAS	MLB	35	1.35	4.53	103	0.1	94.8	59.9%	20.4%	53.0%

Javy Guerra, continued

Pitch Shape vs LHH

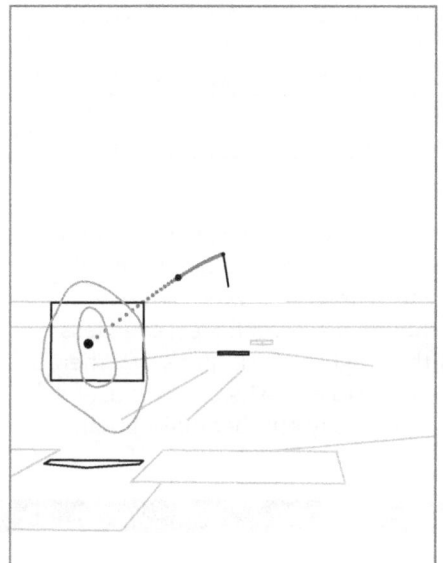

Pitch Shape vs RHH

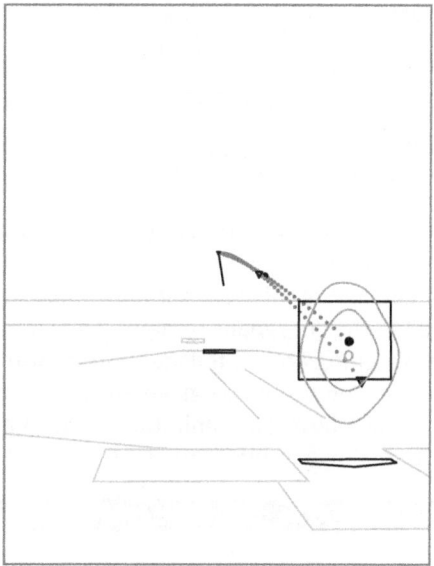

Type	Frequency	Velocity	H Movement	V Movement
● Fastball	67.0%	92 [98]	-2.6 [120]	-11.4 [111]
▲ Changeup	7.7%	84.4 [97]	-7.2 [124]	-23.1 [112]
▽ Slider	15.4%	85.9 [109]	5.3 [100]	-27.9 [117]
◇ Curveball	8.4%	79 [102]	4 [86]	-46.2 [105]

Washington Nationals 2021

Ryne Harper   RHP
Born: 03/27/89   Age: 32   Bats: R   Throws: R
Height: 6'3"   Weight: 215   Origin: Round 37, 2011 Draft (#1136 overall)

YEAR	TEAM	LVL	AGE	W	L	SV	G	GS	IP	H	HR	BB/9	K/9	K	GB%	BABIP
2018	CHA	AA	29	1	2	6	24	0	39	35	0	1.2	11.8	51	39.2%	.365
2018	ROC	AAA	29	0	3	0	14	0	26	26	2	1.7	12.1	35	60.3%	.364
2019	MIN	MLB	30	4	2	1	61	0	54^1	54	7	1.7	8.3	50	38.0%	.301
2020	WAS	MLB	31	1	0	0	23	0	23^2	29	5	3.4	9.5	25	34.7%	.343
2021 FS	WAS	MLB	32	2	2	0	57	0	50	46	7	2.5	9.1	50	40.0%	.289
2021 DC	WAS	MLB	32	2	2	0	54	0	46.3	43	7	2.5	9.1	47	40.0%	.289

Comparables: Josh Fields, Hunter Strickland, Pat Venditte

    Harper earned his first Annual comment in last year's book. In said comment, we predicted that hitters might grow wise to his curveball-other-curveball arsenal. That might eventually prove to be the case, but it wasn't true in 2020—the curveballs remained effective, though his fastball grew even less threatening and he finished the season with an ugly ERA. Harper's peripherals suggest he should be given another opportunity to prove he can be a useful middle reliever; at minimum, his surname and jersey number make for an interesting combination in D.C.

YEAR	TEAM	LVL	AGE	WHIP	ERA	DRA-	WARP	MPH	FB%	WHF	CSP
2018	CHA	AA	29	1.03	2.54	58	1.0				
2018	ROC	AAA	29	1.19	5.19	57	0.7				
2019	MIN	MLB	30	1.18	3.81	95	0.4	91.0	38.7%	23.9%	
2020	WAS	MLB	31	1.61	7.61	104	0.2	89.9	38.1%	20.4%	
2021 FS	WAS	MLB	32	1.20	3.70	87	0.6	90.5	38.5%	22.4%	52.1%
2021 DC	WAS	MLB	32	1.20	3.70	87	0.6	90.5	38.5%	22.4%	52.1%

Ryne Harper, continued

Pitch Shape vs LHH

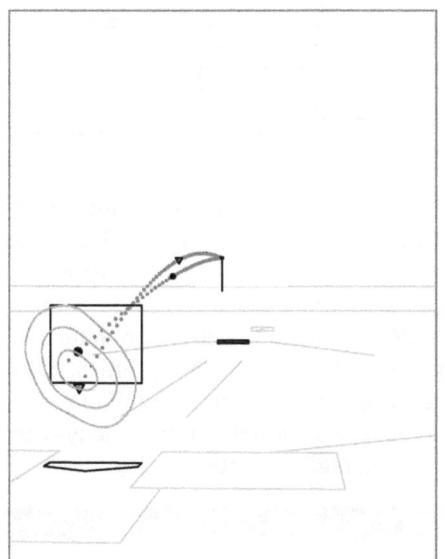

Pitch Shape vs RHH

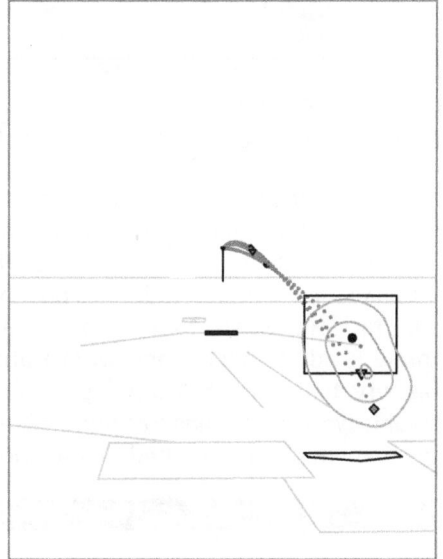

Type	Frequency	Velocity	H Movement	V Movement
● Fastball	37.1%	88.6 [87]	0 [132]	-21.3 [83]
▽ Slider	47.9%	75 [60]	11.3 [123]	-49.2 [55]
◇ Curveball	11.9%	69.6 [65]	11 [114]	-62.1 [69]

Washington Nationals 2021

Will Harris RHP
Born: 08/28/84 Age: 36 Bats: R Throws: R
Height: 6'4" Weight: 240 Origin: Round 9, 2006 Draft (#258 overall)

YEAR	TEAM	LVL	AGE	W	L	SV	G	GS	IP	H	HR	BB/9	K/9	K	GB%	BABIP
2018	HOU	MLB	33	5	3	0	61	0	56^2	48	3	2.2	10.2	64	52.0%	.308
2019	HOU	MLB	34	4	1	4	68	0	60	42	6	2.1	9.3	62	52.9%	.247
2020	WAS	MLB	35	0	1	1	20	0	17^2	21	3	4.6	10.7	21	42.6%	.353
2021 FS	WAS	MLB	36	2	2	6	57	0	50	44	5	3.1	9.5	52	49.2%	.296
2021 DC	WAS	MLB	36	2	2	6	54	0	52.3	47	5	3.1	9.5	55	49.2%	.296

Comparables: Heath Bell, Trevor Hoffman, Tom Henke

If you can't beat 'em, join 'em. Harris' five years in Houston ended not with a whimper, but a clang—a cutter low and away to Howie Kendrick that ricocheted off the foul pole for the World-Series-winning home-run. Harris once again ran into bad luck with the Nationals, posting a respectable ERA but a career-high walk rate. He issued more free passes in 2020 than he did in 2017, when he threw 28 additional innings. Woof. Harris was particularly beset by lefties, with his curveball generating a swing rate of nearly 60 percent...and a whiff rate of 16. Double woof. Harris has two more years to go as a National, but his legacy with the team might be confined to that one autumn night in Houston.

YEAR	TEAM	LVL	AGE	WHIP	ERA	DRA-	WARP	MPH	FB%	WHF	CSP
2018	HOU	MLB	33	1.09	3.49	51	1.7	93.5	62.2%	32.4%	
2019	HOU	MLB	34	0.93	1.50	70	1.2	92.8	58.0%	29.8%	
2020	WAS	MLB	35	1.70	3.06	85	0.3	92.4	77.7%	28.9%	
2021 FS	WAS	MLB	36	1.25	3.48	82	0.8	92.8	64.5%	30.2%	43.8%
2021 DC	WAS	MLB	36	1.25	3.48	82	0.8	92.8	64.5%	30.2%	43.8%

Will Harris, continued

Pitch Shape vs LHH

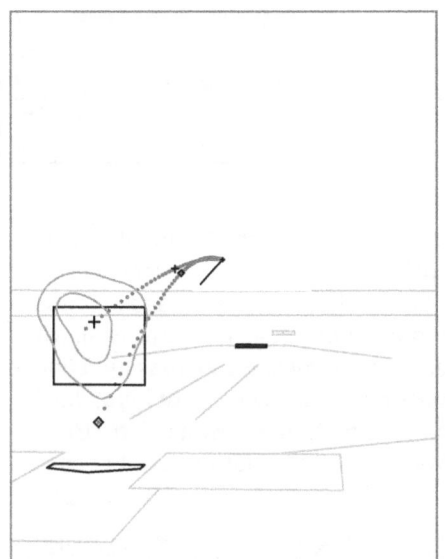

Pitch Shape vs RHH

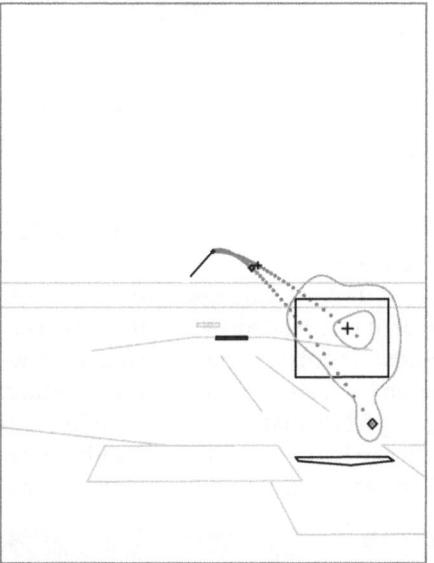

Type	Frequency	Velocity	H Movement	V Movement
+ Cutter	77.7%	90.7 [115]	3.5 [111]	-19.9 [117]
◇ Curveball	22.3%	81 [109]	9.9 [109]	-50.8 [95]

Washington Nationals 2021

Daniel Hudson   RHP
Born: 03/09/87   Age: 34   Bats: R   Throws: R
Height: 6'3"   Weight: 215   Origin: Round 5, 2008 Draft (#150 overall)

YEAR	TEAM	LVL	AGE	W	L	SV	G	GS	IP	H	HR	BB/9	K/9	K	GB%	BABIP
2018	LAD	MLB	31	3	2	0	40	1	46	38	6	3.5	8.6	44	38.2%	.256
2019	WAS	MLB	32	3	0	6	24	0	25	18	3	1.4	8.3	23	27.5%	.227
2019	TOR	MLB	32	6	3	2	45	1	48	38	5	4.3	9.0	48	41.4%	.260
2020	WAS	MLB	33	3	2	10	21	0	20^2	15	6	4.8	12.2	28	18.0%	.209
2021 FS	WAS	MLB	34	2	2	14	57	0	50	44	8	3.9	9.8	54	34.7%	.284
2021 DC	WAS	MLB	34	2	2	14	54	0	52.3	46	8	3.9	9.8	57	34.7%	.284

Comparables: Wade Davis, David Phelps, Mark Guthrie

A little-known addendum to the MLB rules dictate that the Nationals must overuse a fastball-heavy reliever at some point. In 2019, that reliever was Doolittle, who was asked to carry a leaky bullpen for much of the season; last year, it was Hudson's turn to serve as a fireman. It didn't go nearly as well, with Hudson contributing more fuel than water to the flames. His increasing reliance upon his fastball makes sense—it still tempts hitters to swing—but his slider going from missable to miserable made him ineffectual. Hudson will try to salvage his career for, oh, the fifth or so time in 2021. No matter how it goes, Nationals fans will always have Houston.

YEAR	TEAM	LVL	AGE	WHIP	ERA	DRA-	WARP	MPH	FB%	WHF	CSP
2018	LAD	MLB	31	1.22	4.11	103	0.2	96.8	54.4%	28.4%	
2019	WAS	MLB	32	0.88	1.44	77	0.4	97.6	72.4%	22.4%	
2019	TOR	MLB	32	1.27	3.00	104	0.1	97.2	70.2%	23.2%	
2020	WAS	MLB	33	1.26	6.10	124	-0.1	97.9	75.9%	31.2%	
2021 FS	WAS	MLB	34	1.32	4.32	97	0.3	97.4	69.5%	26.1%	50.5%
2021 DC	WAS	MLB	34	1.32	4.32	97	0.3	97.4	69.5%	26.1%	50.5%

Daniel Hudson, continued

Pitch Shape vs LHH

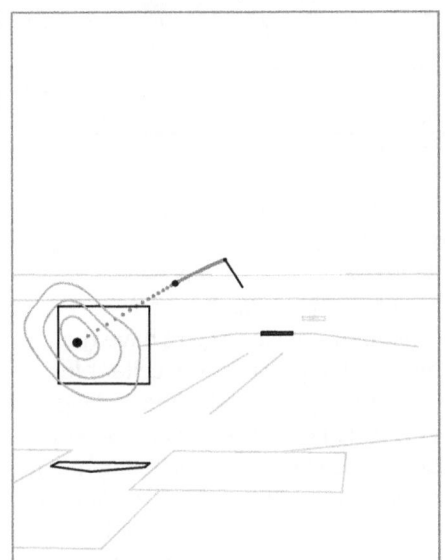

Pitch Shape vs RHH

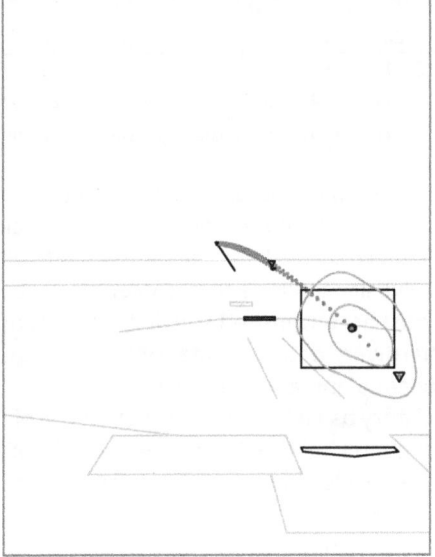

Type	Frequency	Velocity	H Movement	V Movement
● Fastball	75.9%	96.7 [113]	-8.7 [91]	-11.4 [111]
▲ Changeup	5.6%	88.4 [113]	-15.5 [80]	-23.5 [111]
▽ Slider	16.7%	86.2 [110]	1.9 [87]	-31.7 [106]

Washington Nationals 2021

Jon Lester LHP
Born: 01/07/84   Age: 37   Bats: L   Throws: L
Height: 6'4"   Weight: 240   Origin: Round 2, 2002 Draft (#57 overall)

YEAR	TEAM	LVL	AGE	W	L	SV	G	GS	IP	H	HR	BB/9	K/9	K	GB%	BABIP
2018	CHC	MLB	34	18	6	0	32	32	181²	174	24	3.2	7.4	149	38.0%	.294
2019	CHC	MLB	35	13	10	0	31	31	171²	205	26	2.7	8.7	165	42.3%	.350
2020	CHC	MLB	36	3	3	0	12	12	61	64	11	2.5	6.2	42	47.8%	.277
2021 FS	WAS	MLB	37	9	9	0	26	26	150	154	23	3.2	7.3	122	45.0%	.295
2021 DC	WAS	MLB	37	8	8	0	25	25	139.7	144	21	3.2	7.3	114	45.0%	.295

Comparables: Aníbal Sánchez, Zack Greinke, Justin Verlander

    Cinematic history is littered with stories of once-great virtuosos clinging desperately to greatness, or going back for one last run at glory: *Sunset Boulevard, Birdman, Incredibles, A Mighty Wind* (sort of), basically every Sylvester Stallone movie ever made. Lester entered the season as one of the most accomplished starting pitchers of his generation. He doesn't have the hardware of a Verlander or Kershaw, but he's been consistently excellent for a decade and a half and he has the eighth most innings pitched in major-league history as well as the distinct honor of having pitched for three World Series winners. So, that there was a legitimate case for the Cubs to *avoid* using him in the postseason says a lot. It never came to that, as the Cubs lost to the Marlins in two games, but Lester's slow, age-related decline seemed to speed up last season: He stopped missing bats, gave up a whole lot of hard contact and essentially turned every opposite-handed batter who came to the plate into the AL Rookie of the Year. This is clearly Lester's swan song, and even if it doesn't turn out quite like *Uncle Drew*, it would probably make for a better movie.

YEAR	TEAM	LVL	AGE	WHIP	ERA	DRA-	WARP	MPH	FB%	WHF	CSP
2018	CHC	MLB	34	1.31	3.32	99	1.8	92.7	50.3%	20.5%	
2019	CHC	MLB	35	1.50	4.46	114	0.3	92.2	38.8%	21.3%	
2020	CHC	MLB	36	1.33	5.16	133	-0.5	90.9	41.2%	18.2%	
2021 FS	WAS	MLB	37	1.39	4.64	105	1.0	92.0	42.3%	20.3%	45.7%
2021 DC	WAS	MLB	37	1.39	4.64	105	1.0	92.0	42.3%	20.3%	45.7%

Jon Lester, continued

Pitch Shape vs LHH

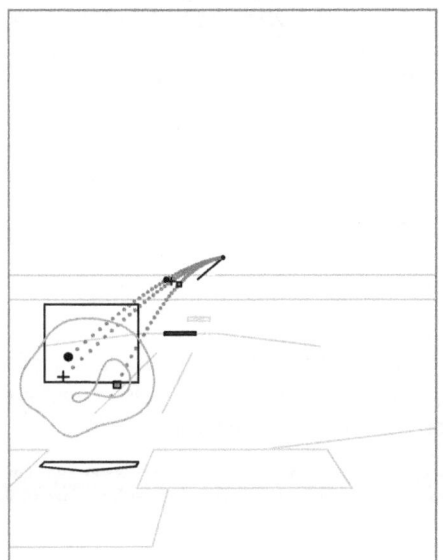

Pitch Shape vs RHH

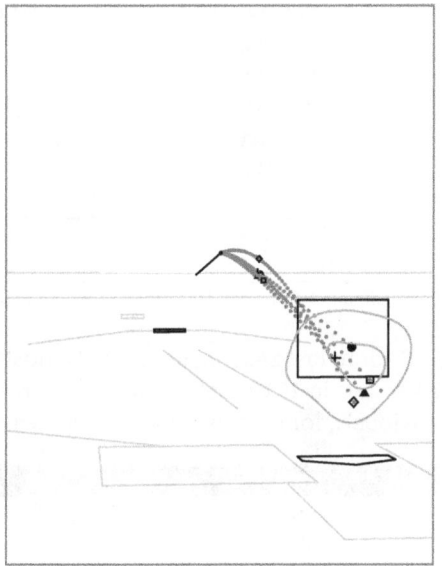

Type	Frequency	Velocity	H Movement	V Movement
● Fastball	27.1%	89.6 [91]	6.6 [100]	-16.5 [96]
□ Sinker	14.1%	88.8 [81]	12.1 [107]	-24.5 [87]
+ Cutter	32.5%	87.6 [95]	-0.4 [90]	-21.8 [110]
▲ Changeup	13.5%	83.6 [94]	11.9 [99]	-28.9 [96]
◇ Curveball	12.8%	73.6 [80]	-9.5 [108]	-49.6 [97]

Kyle McGowin RHP

Born: 11/27/91 Age: 29 Bats: R Throws: R
Height: 6'3" Weight: 195 Origin: Round 5, 2013 Draft (#157 overall)

YEAR	TEAM	LVL	AGE	W	L	SV	G	GS	IP	H	HR	BB/9	K/9	K	GB%	BABIP
2018	FBG	HI-A	26	1	1	0	2	2	11	8	2	2.5	11.5	14	38.5%	.250
2018	HBG	AA	26	4	3	0	13	13	78	62	7	2.2	10.8	94	47.8%	.284
2018	SYR	AAA	26	3	2	0	8	8	52²	26	3	1.5	7.5	44	43.6%	.177
2018	WAS	MLB	26	0	0	0	5	1	7²	6	2	5.9	9.4	8	33.3%	.211
2019	HBG	AA	27	1	1	0	6	6	32¹	22	2	2.5	10.0	36	38.5%	.263
2019	FRE	AAA	27	7	2	0	11	11	60²	59	8	2.5	10.1	68	46.1%	.323
2019	WAS	MLB	27	0	0	1	7	1	16	22	7	2.2	10.1	18	43.4%	.333
2020	WAS	MLB	28	1	0	1	9	0	11	9	2	4.1	13.1	16	38.5%	.292
2021 FS	*WAS*	*MLB*	*29*	*2*	*2*	*0*	*57*	*0*	*50*	*44*	*7*	*3.4*	*9.8*	*54*	*41.5%*	*.291*
2021 DC	*WAS*	*MLB*	*29*	*2*	*2*	*0*	*48*	*0*	*40.7*	*36*	*6*	*3.4*	*9.8*	*44*	*41.5%*	*.291*

Comparables: Austin Voth, Luis Cessa, Glenn Sparkman

Prior to last season, McGowin's most notable feat as a big-leaguer was a May 24th start in 2019 that marked the turning point of the Nationals season—albeit, obviously, for reasons beyond his own doing. That's still the case.

YEAR	TEAM	LVL	AGE	WHIP	ERA	DRA-	WARP	MPH	FB%	WHF	CSP
2018	FBG	HI-A	26	1.00	4.09	96	0.1				
2018	HBG	AA	26	1.04	3.69	54	2.5				
2018	SYR	AAA	26	0.66	1.20	66	1.4				
2018	WAS	MLB	26	1.43	5.87	103	0.0	92.4	59.2%	33.3%	
2019	HBG	AA	27	0.96	2.51	66	0.7				
2019	FRE	AAA	27	1.25	3.86	63	2.1				
2019	WAS	MLB	27	1.62	10.12	74	0.3	92.8	52.7%	30.0%	
2020	WAS	MLB	28	1.27	4.91	85	0.2	92.9	28.1%	38.5%	
2021 FS	*WAS*	*MLB*	*29*	*1.28*	*3.97*	*91*	*0.5*	*92.8*	*42.2%*	*34.2%*	*43.8%*
2021 DC	*WAS*	*MLB*	*29*	*1.28*	*3.97*	*91*	*0.4*	*92.8*	*42.2%*	*34.2%*	*43.8%*

Kyle McGowin, continued

Pitch Shape vs LHH	Pitch Shape vs RHH
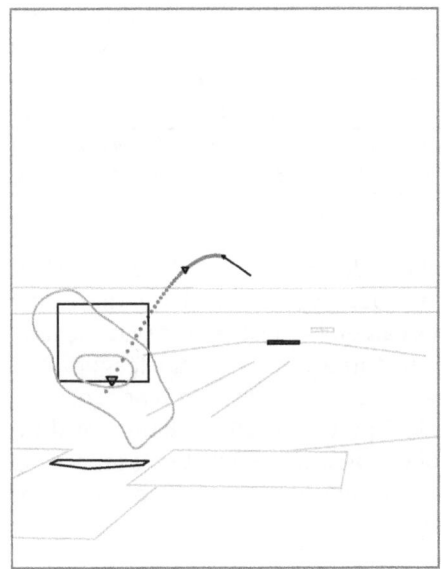	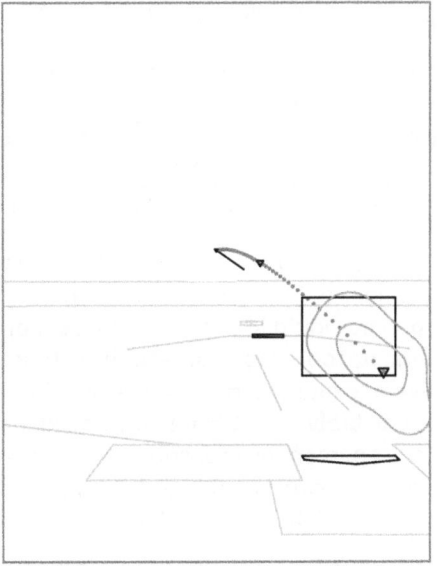

Type	Frequency	Velocity	H Movement	V Movement
● Fastball	11.9%	91.7 [97]	-6.3 [102]	-13.6 [104]
□ Sinker	15.9%	91.3 [94]	-13.7 [95]	-19.6 [103]
▽ Slider	70.6%	82.1 [92]	7.7 [109]	-35.8 [94]

Washington Nationals 2021

Tanner Rainey   RHP
Born: 12/25/92   Age: 28   Bats: R   Throws: R
Height: 6'2"   Weight: 235   Origin: Round 2, 2015 Draft (#71 overall)

YEAR	TEAM	LVL	AGE	W	L	SV	G	GS	IP	H	HR	BB/9	K/9	K	GB%	BABIP
2018	LOU	AAA	25	7	2	3	44	0	51	25	2	6.2	11.5	65	35.2%	.225
2018	CIN	MLB	25	0	0	0	8	0	7	13	4	15.4	9.0	7	30.8%	.409
2019	FRE	AAA	26	2	2	2	16	0	18	16	1	6.0	16.0	32	56.8%	.417
2019	WAS	MLB	26	2	3	0	52	0	48^1	32	6	7.1	13.6	73	51.0%	.286
2020	WAS	MLB	27	1	1	0	20	0	20^1	8	4	3.1	14.2	32	34.3%	.129
2021 FS	WAS	MLB	28	2	2	0	57	0	50	37	6	6.3	13.5	75	43.3%	.303
2021 DC	WAS	MLB	28	2	2	0	54	0	46.3	35	5	6.3	13.5	69	43.3%	.303

Comparables: John Curtiss, Dan Altavilla, Dovydas Neverauskas

Baseball advice usually boils down to platitudes, whether it's "see the ball, hit the ball" or "just throw strikes." Rainey has probably heard the latter more often than he would like to admit throughout his career, but last season was the first time he took it to heart—to the extent that he threw more than the league-average rate of strikes, something inconceivable as recently as a year ago. Predictably, his walk rate improved: from 17.8 percent in 2019, all the way down to 9.3 percent last season. Rainey's control was about the only thing separating him from consistent high-leverage work; if his gains prove sustainable, don't be surprised if he starts racking up saves sooner than later.

YEAR	TEAM	LVL	AGE	WHIP	ERA	DRA-	WARP	MPH	FB%	WHF	CSP
2018	LOU	AAA	25	1.18	2.65	72	0.9				
2018	CIN	MLB	25	3.57	24.43	201	-0.3	99.7	71.4%	29.9%	
2019	FRE	AAA	26	1.56	4.00	54	0.6				
2019	WAS	MLB	26	1.45	3.91	62	1.2	99.4	70.8%	40.7%	
2020	WAS	MLB	27	0.74	2.66	77	0.4	98.6	60.9%	47.3%	
2021 FS	WAS	MLB	28	1.46	4.28	93	0.4	99.2	67.7%	42.0%	43.8%
2021 DC	WAS	MLB	28	1.46	4.28	93	0.4	99.2	67.7%	42.0%	43.8%

Tanner Rainey, continued

Pitch Shape vs LHH

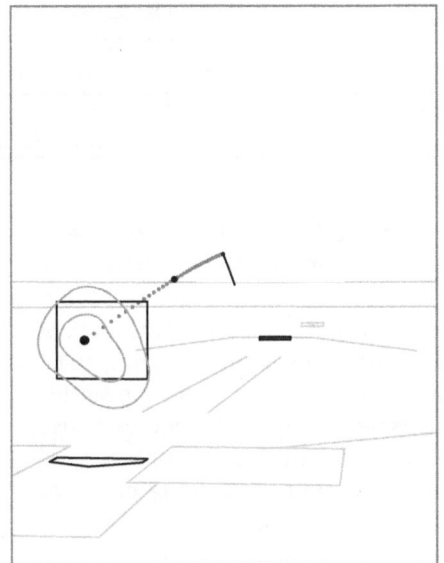

Pitch Shape vs RHH

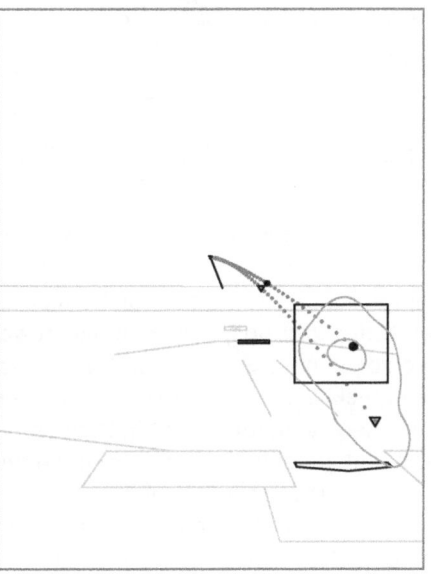

Type	Frequency	Velocity	H Movement	V Movement
● Fastball	60.1%	96.8 [113]	-5.5 [106]	-10.6 [113]
▽ Slider	38.6%	87.3 [115]	3.6 [94]	-34.2 [99]

Aníbal Sánchez RHP
Born: 02/27/84   Age: 37   Bats: R   Throws: R
Height: 6'0"   Weight: 205   Origin: International Free Agent, 2001

YEAR	TEAM	LVL	AGE	W	L	SV	G	GS	IP	H	HR	BB/9	K/9	K	GB%	BABIP
2018	GWN	AAA	34	0	1	0	2	2	6^2	9	2	5.4	12.2	9	21.1%	.412
2018	ATL	MLB	34	7	6	0	25	24	136^2	106	15	2.8	8.9	135	44.1%	.260
2019	WAS	MLB	35	11	8	0	30	30	166	153	22	3.1	7.3	134	38.0%	.266
2020	WAS	MLB	36	4	5	0	11	11	53	70	11	3.1	7.3	43	39.8%	.347
2021 FS	WAS	MLB	37	9	8	0	26	26	150	147	23	2.8	7.4	122	39.6%	.283
2021 DC	WAS	MLB	37	7	7	0	23	23	115	112	18	2.8	7.4	94	39.6%	.283

Comparables: Wandy Rodriguez, Ted Lilly, Kevin Appier

    A quirk of butterfly biology: Most monarch butterflies live for a few mere weeks in the summer. But a monarch "super-generation" migrates from their reproduction sites in the northern parts of the United States and Canada to their wintering grounds, only to make the same journey in reverse months later. So too go pitchers. Some emerge with flashes of brilliance in the heat, only to cycle out quickly. Others persist. Sánchez certainly has, first as a star for the Marlins and then again for Detroit in their early-2010s heyday. He then remade himself as a junkballer with seven(ish) pitch types, including the slow, flapping mariposa (butterfly) changeup. Even super-monarchs have to hang 'em up at some point, and Sánchez may be at that point, having watched his ERA and peripherals all transform from solid to marginal last season. Still, if anyone is going to reinvent themselves once more, it's probably the pitcher who is familiar with metamorphosis—as with anything else, the more you do it, the better you know how to.

YEAR	TEAM	LVL	AGE	WHIP	ERA	DRA-	WARP	MPH	FB%	WHF	CSP
2018	GWN	AAA	34	1.95	10.80	55	0.2				
2018	ATL	MLB	34	1.08	2.83	61	4.0	92.7	37.6%	25.2%	
2019	WAS	MLB	35	1.27	3.85	90	2.5	92.4	35.1%	22.5%	
2020	WAS	MLB	36	1.66	6.62	123	-0.2	91.6	32.6%	23.7%	
2021 FS	WAS	MLB	37	1.29	4.10	97	1.7	92.3	34.9%	23.4%	45.9%
2021 DC	WAS	MLB	37	1.29	4.10	97	1.3	92.3	34.9%	23.4%	45.9%

Aníbal Sánchez, continued

Pitch Shape vs LHH

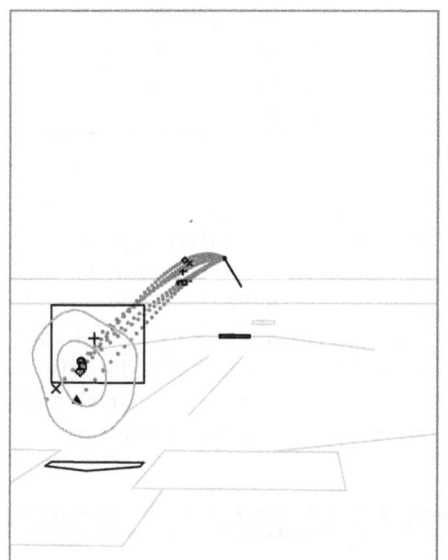

Pitch Shape vs RHH

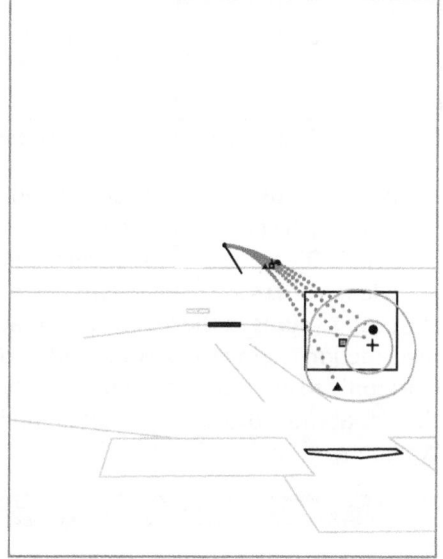

Type		Frequency	Velocity	H Movement	V Movement
●	Fastball	25.0%	89.6 [91]	-5.2 [107]	-15.1 [100]
□	Sinker	7.5%	89.8 [86]	-11.4 [112]	-17.6 [110]
+	Cutter	24.4%	87.9 [97]	-0.1 [87]	-20.3 [115]
▲	Changeup	29.0%	82 [88]	-12.4 [97]	-30.6 [91]
×	Splitter	6.5%	69.8 [29]	-8.4 [98]	-45.1 [48]
◇	Curveball	6.1%	76.3 [91]	3.6 [84]	-43.6 [111]

Washington Nationals 2021

Max Scherzer RHP
Born: 07/27/84 Age: 36 Bats: R Throws: R
Height: 6'3" Weight: 215 Origin: Round 1, 2006 Draft (#11 overall)

YEAR	TEAM	LVL	AGE	W	L	SV	G	GS	IP	H	HR	BB/9	K/9	K	GB%	BABIP
2018	WAS	MLB	33	18	7	0	33	33	220^2	150	23	2.1	12.2	300	34.2%	.267
2019	WAS	MLB	34	11	7	0	27	27	172^1	144	18	1.7	12.7	243	40.8%	.322
2020	WAS	MLB	35	5	4	0	12	12	67^1	70	10	3.1	12.3	92	33.0%	.355
2021 FS	WAS	MLB	36	10	6	0	26	26	150	122	20	2.2	11.3	187	36.3%	.290
2021 DC	WAS	MLB	36	12	7	0	29	29	174.7	143	23	2.2	11.3	219	36.3%	.290

Comparables: Jake Peavy, Zack Greinke, Roger Clemens

Pity Odysseus so long at sea; cursed by Poseidon to misadventure and misfortune, his possibility of return 20 years denied. Scherzer's own journey to baseball's Olympus seemed itself snakebit. A 2012 World Series loss. A 2013 ALCS loss. A 2014 ALDS loss. Two more NLDS losses with the Nationals. A brief stint as a cyclops in the legendary "black eye" game. A metaphorical death and resurrection during the 2019 World Series, felled by a neck injury and a delayed start, only to emerge victorious. So pity Scherzer, now home, cursed to sit and think that most troublesome question for heroes long-returned from war: Well...now what?

YEAR	TEAM	LVL	AGE	WHIP	ERA	DRA-	WARP	MPH	FB%	WHF	CSP
2018	WAS	MLB	33	0.91	2.53	51	7.7	96.5	50.1%	33.4%	
2019	WAS	MLB	34	1.03	2.92	50	6.2	96.9	48.3%	34.0%	
2020	WAS	MLB	35	1.38	3.74	79	1.3	96.8	46.0%	32.6%	
2021 FS	WAS	MLB	36	1.06	2.89	70	4.0	96.8	48.1%	33.4%	49.1%
2021 DC	WAS	MLB	36	1.06	2.89	70	4.6	96.8	48.1%	33.4%	49.1%

Max Scherzer, continued

Pitch Shape vs LHH

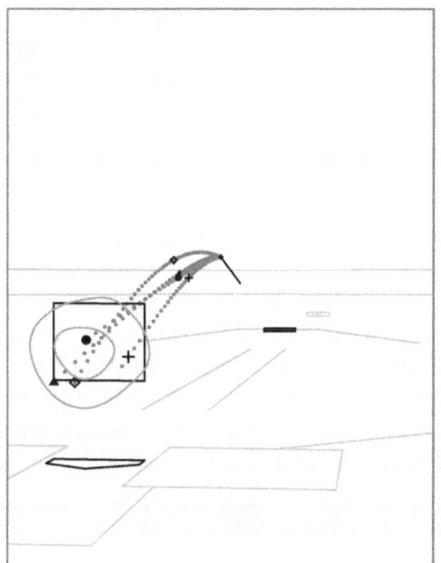

Pitch Shape vs RHH

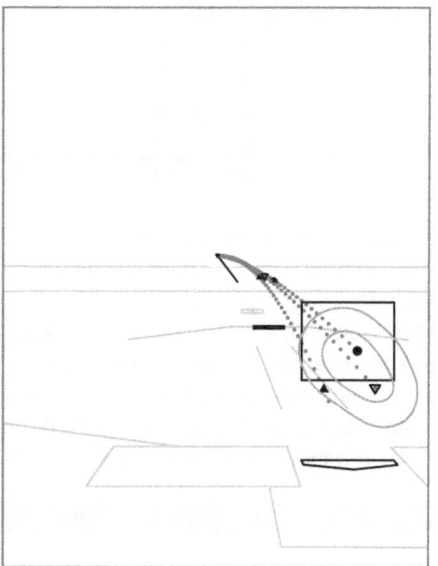

Type	Frequency	Velocity	H Movement	V Movement
● Fastball	45.9%	94.9 [107]	-9.3 [88]	-13.5 [105]
+ Cutter	9.8%	91.3 [119]	-0.5 [84]	-21.4 [111]
▲ Changeup	16.0%	85.1 [100]	-12.8 [94]	-31.4 [89]
▽ Slider	18.9%	85.6 [108]	3.7 [94]	-31.2 [107]
◇ Curveball	9.1%	77.4 [95]	12.9 [121]	-49.3 [98]

Washington Nationals 2021

Wander Suero RHP
Born: 09/15/91   Age: 29   Bats: R   Throws: R
Height: 6'4"   Weight: 211   Origin: International Free Agent, 2010

YEAR	TEAM	LVL	AGE	W	L	SV	G	GS	IP	H	HR	BB/9	K/9	K	GB%	BABIP
2018	SYR	AAA	26	1	2	1	14	0	17	16	1	2.1	8.5	16	46.0%	.306
2018	WAS	MLB	26	4	1	0	40	0	47^2	43	4	2.8	8.9	47	34.3%	.302
2019	WAS	MLB	27	6	9	1	78	0	71^1	64	5	3.3	10.2	81	40.3%	.326
2020	WAS	MLB	28	2	0	0	22	0	23^2	20	1	3.8	10.6	28	37.7%	.317
2021 FS	WAS	MLB	29	2	2	0	57	0	50	45	7	3.4	9.9	54	38.8%	.296
2021 DC	WAS	MLB	29	2	2	0	54	0	46.3	42	6	3.4	9.9	51	38.8%	.296

Comparables: Cam Bedrosian, Dominic Leone, Zach Putnam

If single-pitch relievers are defined as players who throw the same pitch type more than 80 percent of the time, then the 2020 Nationals improbably boasted two such players: Doolittle and Suero. Suero's cutter usage even exceeded Kenley Jansen's—Jansen's cut baseballs at a career-low rate while Suero opted for the other direction, mothballing his curveball in the process. Of particular note, Suero fared much better last year than this against lefties, even though he faced them more frequently in 2020. That's a promising potential development if he wants to remain more than the Nationals' designated rubber arm.

YEAR	TEAM	LVL	AGE	WHIP	ERA	DRA-	WARP	MPH	FB%	WHF	CSP
2018	SYR	AAA	26	1.18	3.71	67	0.3				
2018	WAS	MLB	26	1.22	3.59	95	0.3	94.0	79.9%	24.6%	
2019	WAS	MLB	27	1.26	4.54	74	1.3	95.1	72.1%	29.4%	
2020	WAS	MLB	28	1.27	3.80	86	0.4	93.8	81.1%	32.7%	
2021 FS	WAS	MLB	29	1.29	4.07	92	0.5	94.6	75.9%	29.4%	49.2%
2021 DC	WAS	MLB	29	1.29	4.07	92	0.4	94.6	75.9%	29.4%	49.2%

Wander Suero, continued

Pitch Shape vs LHH

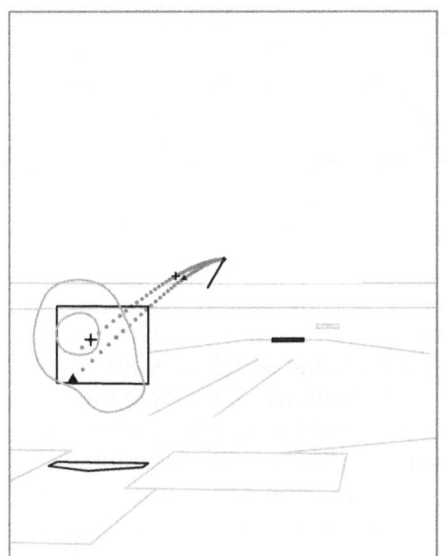

Pitch Shape vs RHH

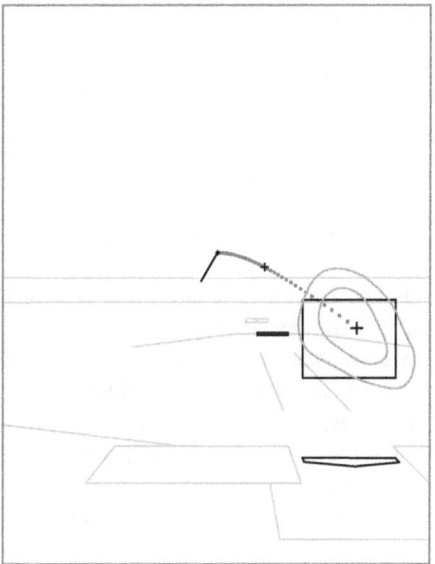

Type	Frequency	Velocity	H Movement	V Movement
+ Cutter	79.4%	91.2 [118]	2.1 [101]	-17.9 [125]
▲ Changeup	13.4%	86.4 [105]	-10.9 [104]	-27.5 [100]
◇ Curveball	5.1%	77.2 [95]	11.4 [116]	-53.3 [89]

Washington Nationals 2021

Austin Voth RHP
Born: 06/26/92   Age: 29   Bats: R   Throws: R
Height: 6'2"   Weight: 210   Origin: Round 5, 2013 Draft (#166 overall)

YEAR	TEAM	LVL	AGE	W	L	SV	G	GS	IP	H	HR	BB/9	K/9	K	GB%	BABIP
2018	SYR	AAA	26	6	8	0	24	24	125²	119	13	2.9	8.4	117	40.6%	.298
2018	WAS	MLB	26	1	1	0	4	2	12¹	12	3	4.4	8.0	11	42.1%	.265
2019	HBG	AA	27	1	1	0	3	3	11¹	11	1	1.6	8.7	11	36.7%	.345
2019	FRE	AAA	27	3	5	0	12	12	61¹	68	7	2.2	10.0	68	40.8%	.345
2019	WAS	MLB	27	2	1	0	9	8	43²	33	5	2.7	9.1	44	36.8%	.259
2020	WAS	MLB	28	2	5	0	11	11	49²	57	14	3.3	8.0	44	29.6%	.297
2021 FS	WAS	MLB	29	9	9	0	26	26	150	145	29	3.2	8.2	136	34.7%	.279
2021 DC	WAS	MLB	29	6	6	0	40	14	84.3	82	16	3.2	8.2	77	34.7%	.279

Comparables: Alec Mills, Mike Wright, Chris Stratton

Mike Rizzo likes to say that starting pitching wins championships. It certainly worked for the Nationals in 2019, riding four reliable starters (and two bullpen arms) to ascend to baseball's highest peak. It's unclear what Voth's pitching is going to win him or anyone else, other than, perhaps, a ticket back to the minors. His cutter and curve didn't fool hitters, and his ability to find the zone at all wavered. But given the shortened season, dearth of usable arms and the vacancies created by Strasburg and Ross, Voth was nonetheless able to make it through the year without losing his rotation spot. Don't expect that to remain the case heading into 2021.

YEAR	TEAM	LVL	AGE	WHIP	ERA	DRA-	WARP	MPH	FB%	WHF	CSP
2018	SYR	AAA	26	1.27	4.37	92	1.4				
2018	WAS	MLB	26	1.46	6.57	114	0.0	93.0	62.0%	22.0%	
2019	HBG	AA	27	1.15	4.76	114	-0.1				
2019	FRE	AAA	27	1.35	4.40	75	1.8				
2019	WAS	MLB	27	1.05	3.30	83	0.8	94.6	60.5%	28.8%	
2020	WAS	MLB	28	1.51	6.34	159	-1.1	93.6	60.8%	22.2%	
2021 FS	WAS	MLB	29	1.33	4.70	107	0.9	93.9	60.8%	24.3%	49.6%
2021 DC	WAS	MLB	29	1.33	4.70	107	0.4	93.9	60.8%	24.3%	49.6%

Austin Voth, continued

Pitch Shape vs LHH	Pitch Shape vs RHH
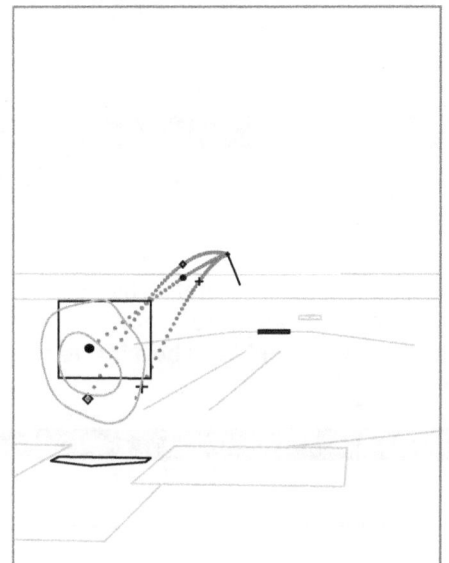	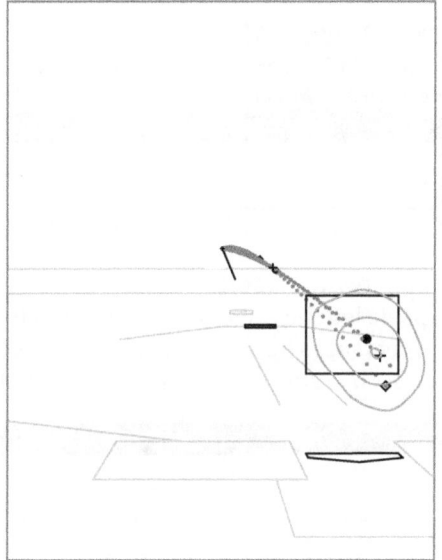

Type	Frequency	Velocity	H Movement	V Movement
● Fastball	60.2%	92.2 [99]	-5.4 [106]	-14.1 [103]
+ Cutter	12.1%	86.8 [91]	1.3 [96]	-25 [97]
◇ Curveball	23.3%	78.5 [99]	12.2 [119]	-44 [110]

PLAYER COMMENTS WITHOUT GRAPHS

Yasel Antuna SS
Born: 10/26/99 Age: 21 Bats: S Throws: R
Height: 6'0" Weight: 170 Origin: International Free Agent, 2016

YEAR	TEAM	LVL	AGE	PA	R	2B	3B	HR	RBI	BB	K	SB	CS	AVG/OBP/SLG
2018	HAG	LO-A	18	362	44	14	2	6	27	32	79	8	7	.220/.293/.331
2021 FS	WAS	MLB	21	600	49	22	2	10	53	42	172	7	5	.208/.267/.314

Comparables: Andrew Velazquez, Juan Diaz, Delino DeShields

Impressive reports from their alternate site and the sweet siren song of upside led the Nats to add Antuna to their 40-man despite the 370 plate appearances he's managed since the start of 2018. He could still be a future star, a lesson in sunk costs or anything in between.

YEAR	TEAM	LVL	AGE	PA	DRC+	BABIP	BRR	FRAA	WARP
2018	HAG	LO-A	18	362	83	.269	-0.6	SS(67): -8.8, 2B(9): 0.2	-0.9
2021 FS	WAS	MLB	21	600	59	.282	0.4	SS -12, 2B 1	-2.5

Alex Avila C
Born: 01/29/87 Age: 34 Bats: L Throws: R
Height: 5'11" Weight: 210 Origin: Round 5, 2008 Draft (#163 overall)

YEAR	TEAM	LVL	AGE	PA	R	2B	3B	HR	RBI	BB	K	SB	CS	AVG/OBP/SLG
2018	ARI	MLB	31	234	13	6	0	7	20	37	90	0	0	.165/.299/.304
2019	ARI	MLB	32	201	22	8	0	9	24	36	68	1	0	.207/.353/.421
2020	MIN	MLB	33	62	6	2	0	1	2	11	22	0	0	.184/.355/.286
2021 FS	WAS	MLB	34	600	81	18	1	19	66	102	224	1	1	.200/.342/.360
2021 DC	WAS	MLB	34	155	21	4	0	5	17	26	58	0	0	.200/.342/.360

Comparables: Jason Castro, David Ross, Rick Wilkins

YEAR	TEAM	P. COUNT	FRM RUNS	BLK RUNS	THRW RUNS	TOT RUNS
2018	ARI	8064	3.7	0.3	0.0	4.0
2019	ARI	7141	-0.1	2.3	0.7	2.9
2020	MIN	2454	-0.8	0.0	0.0	-0.8
2021	WAS	6012	-3.7	0.3	0.2	-3.2
2021	WAS	6012	-3.7	0.3	0.2	-3.1

Casual fans who spot Avila's name in the lineup may still harbor a vague impression of him as some kind of All-Star. After a third consecutive dalliance with the Mendoza Line, though, it's clear that the 34-year-old is in the twilight of his career. A good eye, competent glove and solid reputation in the clubhouse should keep him in the league for a couple more years. Wherever he winds up this offseason, he can expect to play most Sunday afternoons and loiter in shin guards the rest of the week. Hey, there are worse gigs.

YEAR	TEAM	LVL	AGE	PA	DRC+	BABIP	BRR	FRAA	WARP
2018	ARI	MLB	31	234	61	.253	-1.4	C(61): 3.2, 1B(3): 0.0, P(1): -0.0	0.2
2019	ARI	MLB	32	201	95	.287	-1.1	C(54): 2.1, P(2): -0.0	1.0
2020	MIN	MLB	33	62	86	.308	0.0	C(22): 0.2	0.0
2021 FS	WAS	MLB	34	600	98	.319	-0.8	C -10, 1B 0	1.2
2021 DC	WAS	MLB	34	155	98	.319	-0.2	C -3	0.2

Emilio Bonifácio OF
Born: 04/23/85 Age: 36 Bats: S Throws: R
Height: 5'10" Weight: 200 Origin: International Free Agent, 2001

YEAR	TEAM	LVL	AGE	PA	R	2B	3B	HR	RBI	BB	K	SB	CS	AVG/OBP/SLG
2019	DUR	AAA	34	288	48	19	3	8	36	25	63	15	6	.286/.353/.475
2020	WAS	MLB	35	3	1	0	0	0	0	0	2	0	1	.000/.000/.000
2021 FS	WAS	MLB	36	600	47	11	2	10	50	40	174	19	6	.189/.249/.277

Comparables: Rich Thompson, Kazuo Matsui, Omar Infante

Bonifácio unexpectedly resurfaced in the majors after three years of bouncing between the minors and the Atlantic League. His return was even shorter than his annual April hot streaks.

Washington Nationals 2021

YEAR	TEAM	LVL	AGE	PA	DRC+	BABIP	BRR	FRAA	WARP
2019	DUR	AAA	34	288	101	.351	2.9	CF(31): -2.8, LF(22): 1.5, SS(12): -0.6	1.1
2020	WAS	MLB	35	3	107	.000	0.0	LF(1): 0.2	0.0
2021 FS	WAS	MLB	36	600	46	.255	2.0	CF -3, LF -1	-2.7

Adrían Sanchez SS
Born: 08/16/90   Age: 30   Bats: R   Throws: R
Height: 6'0"   Weight: 208   Origin: International Free Agent, 2007

YEAR	TEAM	LVL	AGE	PA	R	2B	3B	HR	RBI	BB	K	SB	CS	AVG/OBP/SLG
2018	SYR	AAA	27	295	21	15	2	4	27	16	42	10	6	.234/.281/.349
2018	WAS	MLB	27	59	8	2	1	0	3	1	8	0	0	.276/.288/.345
2019	HBG	AA	28	282	43	19	1	6	36	19	39	11	5	.316/.365/.469
2019	WAS	MLB	28	32	3	0	0	0	1	1	10	0	0	.226/.250/.226
2021 FS	WAS	MLB	30	600	51	24	2	12	57	30	136	6	2	.222/.268/.337

Comparables: Rey Navarro, Melvin Dorta, Niuman Romero

Now 30 years old with all of 166 career major league plate appearances, Sanchez is the ghost that hangs over Wilmer Difo's shoulder, rattling his glove and wailing about a life spent stapled to the bench as a backup infielder with no standout skill beyond being cheap.

YEAR	TEAM	LVL	AGE	PA	DRC+	BABIP	BRR	FRAA	WARP
2018	SYR	AAA	27	295	69	.260	0.3	SS(29): 2.0, 3B(23): -1.9, 2B(19): 1.1	-0.1
2018	WAS	MLB	27	59	87	.320	1.0	2B(13): -1.1, 3B(7): -0.2	0.1
2019	HBG	AA	28	282	156	.349	2.3	2B(33): -0.8, 3B(21): 0.3, SS(18): 1.8	3.0
2019	WAS	MLB	28	32	60	.333	0.6	3B(6): 0.0, 2B(4): -0.0, SS(2): -0.0	0.0
2021 FS	WAS	MLB	30	600	65	.272	-0.1	2B 0, SS 2	-0.9

Andrew Stevenson LF

Born: 06/01/94   Age: 27   Bats: L   Throws: L
Height: 6'0"   Weight: 192   Origin: Round 2, 2015 Draft (#58 overall)

YEAR	TEAM	LVL	AGE	PA	R	2B	3B	HR	RBI	BB	K	SB	CS	AVG/OBP/SLG
2018	SYR	AAA	24	331	40	10	1	6	28	31	75	12	6	.235/.318/.338
2018	WAS	MLB	24	86	9	2	0	1	13	6	23	1	1	.253/.306/.320
2019	HBG	AA	25	88	12	4	0	1	5	3	24	3	0	.250/.284/.333
2019	FRE	AAA	25	333	50	17	8	6	44	24	76	10	4	.334/.383/.503
2019	WAS	MLB	25	37	4	1	1	0	0	6	11	0	1	.367/.486/.467
2020	WAS	MLB	26	47	11	7	1	2	12	5	11	2	0	.366/.447/.732
2021 FS	WAS	MLB	27	600	70	25	4	11	58	46	160	9	4	.240/.305/.367
2021 DC	WAS	MLB	27	345	40	14	2	6	33	26	92	5	2	.240/.305/.367

Comparables: Greg Golson, Choo Freeman, Eric Reed

It took him a while to get going, and the sample size is miniscule, but Stevenson is finally beginning to show the skills that made him a second-round pick. It's not his fault that playing time has been hard to come by, owing to Washington's crowded outfield and propensity for lining the bench with mid-tier veterans, but he hadn't forced the issue either, falling mostly flat when given playing time. That's likely changed after he spent 2020 hitting the ball with real authority, including an enormous jump in exit velocity and hard-hit rate. Granted, we're talking about results from all of 47 plate appearances across 15 games, but with Adam Eaton gone, it would behoove the Nationals to give Stevenson some rope and see what's fact and what's fiction, and whether he can hack it as a regular.

YEAR	TEAM	LVL	AGE	PA	DRC+	BABIP	BRR	FRAA	WARP
2018	SYR	AAA	24	331	84	.296	-1.0	CF(49): -8.3, LF(25): 1.4, RF(4): -0.4	-0.9
2018	WAS	MLB	24	86	69	.333	0.4	LF(16): -1.4, CF(3): -0.3, RF(1): -0.1	-0.2
2019	HBG	AA	25	88	16	.339	1.1	LF(10): 2.5, CF(8): -0.9	-0.1
2019	FRE	AAA	25	333	98	.428	1.5	CF(52): -10.5, LF(12): -1.1, RF(9): 1.1	0.3
2019	WAS	MLB	25	37	75	.579	-0.2	LF(5): -0.7	-0.1
2020	WAS	MLB	26	47	111	.464	-0.4	LF(9): 0.5, RF(4): 0.1, CF(1): 0.1	0.1
2021 FS	WAS	MLB	27	600	83	.320	0.7	CF -2, RF 0	0.4
2021 DC	WAS	MLB	27	345	83	.320	0.4	CF -1, RF 0	0.2

Washington Nationals 2021

Ryan Zimmerman 1B
Born: 09/28/84   Age: 36   Bats: R   Throws: R
Height: 6'3"   Weight: 215   Origin: Round 1, 2005 Draft (#4 overall)

YEAR	TEAM	LVL	AGE	PA	R	2B	3B	HR	RBI	BB	K	SB	CS	AVG/OBP/SLG
2018	WAS	MLB	33	323	33	21	2	13	51	30	55	1	1	.264/.337/.486
2019	WAS	MLB	34	190	20	9	0	6	27	17	39	0	0	.257/.321/.415
2021 FS	WAS	MLB	36	600	71	26	1	20	79	48	150	2	2	.234/.301/.402
2021 DC	WAS	MLB	36	203	24	8	0	7	26	16	50	0	1	.234/.301/.402

Comparables: Eric Chavez, Casey Blake, Adrián Beltré

In 2019, Zimmerman finally got the ending he deserved: the long-elusive World Series title to cap off a 15-year career in which he kept watching everyone else end their drought. That he didn't retire despite a bunch of back problems and an upcoming 35th birthday was a mild surprise, though you can imagine that he very much wanted a chance to take a victory lap, celebrate on Opening Day, do the ring ceremony, all that good stuff. And like everyone else, all his fun 2020 plans were ruined by the COVID-19 pandemic, as he opted out of the season and stayed home with his family. Assuming he decides to come back to baseball in 2021 (and assuming the Nationals re-sign him), this is probably his last hurrah, so while he missed out on the post-title party, hopefully he gets the other ending he deserves: a chance to say goodbye to the fans of the only franchise he's ever known.

YEAR	TEAM	LVL	AGE	PA	DRC+	BABIP	BRR	FRAA	WARP
2018	WAS	MLB	33	323	111	.284	-0.5	1B(73): 1.4	1.0
2019	WAS	MLB	34	190	93	.297	-0.9	1B(44): 1.2	0.2
2021 FS	WAS	MLB	36	600	93	.285	-0.7	1B 0	0.3
2021 DC	WAS	MLB	36	203	93	.285	-0.2	1B 0	0.1

Rogelio Armenteros RHP
Born: 06/30/94 Age: 27 Bats: R Throws: R
Height: 6'1" Weight: 243 Origin: International Free Agent, 2014

YEAR	TEAM	LVL	AGE	W	L	SV	G	GS	IP	H	HR	BB/9	K/9	K	GB%	BABIP
2018	FRE	AAA	24	8	1	1	22	21	118	106	15	3.7	10.2	134	37.2%	.302
2019	RR	AAA	25	6	7	0	19	18	84[1]	90	14	3.3	9.1	85	31.9%	.328
2019	HOU	MLB	25	1	1	1	5	2	18	17	1	2.5	9.0	18	36.5%	.314
2021 FS	*WAS*	*MLB*	*27*	*9*	*8*	*0*	*26*	*26*	*150*	*134*	*24*	*4.1*	*9.2*	*153*	*36.1%*	*.281*
2021 DC	*WAS*	*MLB*	*27*	*3*	*2*	*0*	*26*	*4*	*39.3*	*35*	*6*	*4.1*	*9.2*	*40*	*36.1%*	*.281*

Comparables: Daniel Mengden, Walker Lockett, Drew Anderson

After waiting so long for a spot in Houston's rotation, Armenteros would have been at the front of the queue when holes started to appear, if not for elbow surgery to remove a bone spur. Others jumped the line while he recovered, leaving him waiting once more for an opportunity, one that may now arrive sooner with a change of scenery.

YEAR	TEAM	LVL	AGE	WHIP	ERA	DRA-	WARP	MPH	FB%	WHF	CSP
2018	FRE	AAA	24	1.31	3.74	79	2.5				
2019	RR	AAA	25	1.43	4.80	94	1.7				
2019	HOU	MLB	25	1.22	4.00	107	0.1	94.0	48.3%	25.2%	
2021 FS	*WAS*	*MLB*	*27*	*1.35*	*4.32*	*98*	*1.6*	*94.0*	*48.3%*	*25.2%*	*43.3%*
2021 DC	*WAS*	*MLB*	*27*	*1.35*	*4.32*	*98*	*0.3*	*94.0*	*48.3%*	*25.2%*	*43.3%*

Aaron Barrett RHP
Born: 01/02/88 Age: 33 Bats: R Throws: R
Height: 6'3" Weight: 230 Origin: Round 9, 2010 Draft (#266 overall)

YEAR	TEAM	LVL	AGE	W	L	SV	G	GS	IP	H	HR	BB/9	K/9	K	GB%	BABIP
2018	AUB	SS	30	2	0	0	20	0	20[2]	13	0	3.5	11.3	26	55.8%	.255
2019	HBG	AA	31	0	2	31	50	0	52[1]	39	6	2.8	10.7	62	51.1%	.258
2019	WAS	MLB	31	0	0	0	3	0	2[1]	5	1	15.4	3.9	1	27.3%	.400
2020	WAS	MLB	32	0	0	0	2	0	1[2]	2	0	10.8	5.4	1	60.0%	.400
2021 FS	*WAS*	*MLB*	*33*	*2*	*3*	*0*	*57*	*0*	*50*	*47*	*7*	*5.2*	*9.2*	*50*	*44.6%*	*.295*

Comparables: Brad Boxberger, Nick Vincent, Steve Cishek

Barrett was the feel-good story of the 2019 Nationals, so, if nothing else, he'll always have that moment. He's a slider-sinker guy now after ditching a four-seamer that had nothing on it any more, but how well that works is still TBD.

Washington Nationals 2021

YEAR	TEAM	LVL	AGE	WHIP	ERA	DRA-	WARP	MPH	FB%	WHF	CSP
2018	AUB	SS	30	1.02	1.74	253	-1.6				
2019	HBG	AA	31	1.05	2.75	71	0.7				
2019	WAS	MLB	31	3.86	15.43	85	0.0	92.6	70.6%	15.0%	
2020	WAS	MLB	32	2.40	10.80	99	0.0	91.2	45.2%	0.0%	
2021 FS	*WAS*	*MLB*	*33*	*1.52*	*5.05*	*110*	*0.0*	*92.0*	*60.3%*	*8.9%*	*38.5%*

Cade Cavalli   RHP
Born: 08/14/98   Age: 22   Bats: R   Throws: R
Height: 6'4"   Weight: 226   Origin: Round 1, 2020 Draft (#22 overall)

Tabbed with the 22nd pick of the 2020 draft, Cavalli—a former two-way player who converted to pitching full-time as a sophomore—boasts a lot of upside thanks to a big body and power stuff, including a fastball that touches 98 mph and a pair of plus breaking balls in his curveball and slider. The question will be whether the right-hander can find consistent command and control, as he battled wildness in his first two seasons at Oklahoma before tightening things up in his shortened junior year. That will go a long way toward determining whether Cavalli's future is in the rotation or the bullpen. Washington will almost certainly let him start for now, but future struggles with walks or a pressing need in relief could force the team's hand.

Brad Hand LHP

Born: 03/20/90 Age: 31 Bats: L Throws: L
Height: 6'3" Weight: 215 Origin: Round 2, 2008 Draft (#52 overall)

YEAR	TEAM	LVL	AGE	W	L	SV	G	GS	IP	H	HR	BB/9	K/9	K	GB%	BABIP
2018	SD	MLB	28	2	4	24	41	0	44^1	33	5	3.0	13.2	65	46.5%	.301
2018	CLE	MLB	28	0	1	8	28	0	27^2	19	3	4.2	13.3	41	40.7%	.291
2019	CLE	MLB	29	6	4	34	60	0	57^1	53	6	2.8	13.2	84	27.2%	.364
2020	CLE	MLB	30	2	1	16	23	0	22	13	0	1.6	11.9	29	26.5%	.265
2021 FS	WAS	MLB	31	2	2	20	57	0	50	41	6	3.2	12.0	66	35.5%	.300
2021 DC	WAS	MLB	31	3	2	20	60	0	52.3	43	7	3.2	12.0	70	35.5%	.300

Comparables: Jeurys Familia, Erasmo Ramírez, Liam Hendriks

Hand's struggles over the second half of 2019 initially looked as though they would continue into 2020 and cast a long shadow over the short season. When the White Sox did damage in consecutive bouts in late July, his ERA was a perilous 15.43. Hand fought back and never lost control, allowing a single earned run across August and September to finish with a perfect save record. The Yankees then smashed his streak and launched Cleveland off the postseason stage in what turned out to be his final appearance with the franchise, as his once-reasonable club option was declined. Cleveland might end up looking more smart than cheap in a year's time: Hand's velocity plummeted and his whiff rate went with it, suggesting his shiny ERA and save percentage could well dip next.

YEAR	TEAM	LVL	AGE	WHIP	ERA	DRA-	WARP	MPH	FB%	WHF	CSP
2018	SD	MLB	28	1.08	3.05	70	0.9	96.0	44.3%	33.0%	
2018	CLE	MLB	28	1.16	2.28	77	0.5	95.6	48.1%	31.4%	
2019	CLE	MLB	29	1.24	3.30	86	0.7	94.7	45.8%	30.7%	
2020	CLE	MLB	30	0.77	2.05	91	0.3	93.4	48.1%	24.8%	
2021 FS	WAS	MLB	31	1.18	3.46	80	0.8	94.7	46.4%	29.7%	50.4%
2021 DC	WAS	MLB	31	1.18	3.46	80	0.8	94.7	46.4%	29.7%	50.4%

Washington Nationals 2021

Cole Henry RHP
Born: 07/15/99 Age: 21 Bats: R Throws: R
Height: 6'4" Weight: 211 Origin: Round 2, 2020 Draft (#55 overall)

There's a lot to like about Henry, starting with the big strikeout numbers he put up across two seasons (well, one and change) at LSU, his fastball that sits 92–94 mph and his plus curveball. The stuff to worry about is his health and durability after he missed time his freshman year with arm trouble, including right elbow soreness, as well as his high-effort delivery (though he's made some mechanical changes). That risk was likely the main reason he fell to the second round of the 2020 draft, where the Nationals are hoping that it'll be worth the reward. The ceiling is a mid-rotation starter; the floor is Hunter Harvey. Somewhere in the middle—let's call it Matt Barnes Territory—is probably Henry's fate.

Seth Romero LHP
Born: 04/19/96 Age: 25 Bats: L Throws: L
Height: 6'3" Weight: 240 Origin: Round 1, 2017 Draft (#25 overall)

YEAR	TEAM	LVL	AGE	W	L	SV	G	GS	IP	H	HR	BB/9	K/9	K	GB%	BABIP
2018	HAG	LO-A	22	0	1	0	7	7	25^1	20	3	2.8	12.1	34	42.2%	.279
2020	WAS	MLB	24	0	0	0	3	0	2^2	5	1	10.1	16.9	5	40.0%	.444
2021 FS	WAS	MLB	25	2	2	0	57	0	50	45	7	4.7	9.7	54	42.4%	.294
2021 DC	WAS	MLB	25	3	2	0	34	3	36	33	5	4.7	9.7	39	42.4%	.294

Romero went from "Charlie Sheen in *Major League*" to more of an Eddie Harris vibe, as his fastball and slider seem to have lost some of their zip and bite. Despite never pitching above A ball and being just two years removed from Tommy John surgery, he got the big-league call for a trio of relief appearances and even struck out the first batter he faced (though granted, it was Billy Hamilton). Still, Romero gave up a grand slam to Tomás Nido in the same inning, so there are clearly some bugs in the system, starting with a fastball that sat 92 and some wobbly control. There were also a fair number of swings and misses, so this isn't a lost cause. The thing to watch for in 2021 will be whether he can rediscover the upside that made him a first-rounder.

YEAR	TEAM	LVL	AGE	WHIP	ERA	DRA-	WARP	MPH	FB%	WHF	CSP
2018	HAG	LO-A	22	1.11	3.91	52	0.8				
2020	WAS	MLB	24	3.00	13.50	72	0.1	93.0	42.4%	36.4%	
2021 FS	WAS	MLB	25	1.43	4.59	103	0.1	93.0	42.4%	36.4%	42.8%
2021 DC	WAS	MLB	25	1.43	4.59	103	0.1	93.0	42.4%	36.4%	42.8%

Joe Ross RHP

Born: 05/21/93   Age: 28   Bats: R   Throws: R
Height: 6'4"   Weight: 220   Origin: Round 1, 2011 Draft (#25 overall)

YEAR	TEAM	LVL	AGE	W	L	SV	G	GS	IP	H	HR	BB/9	K/9	K	GB%	BABIP
2018	NAT	ROK	25	0	0	0	2	2	6	0	0	4.5	12.0	8	55.6%	.000
2018	SYR	AAA	25	2	0	0	2	2	112^{2}	12	0	3.1	3.1	4	43.2%	.273
2018	WAS	MLB	25	0	2	0	3	3	16	17	3	2.2	3.9	7	36.4%	.269
2019	FRE	AAA	26	2	3	0	8	8	40	48	2	1.8	7.2	32	45.7%	.380
2019	WAS	MLB	26	4	4	0	27	9	64	74	7	4.6	8.0	57	43.8%	.351
2021 FS	WAS	MLB	28	9	9	0	26	26	150	149	23	3.5	7.8	130	43.6%	.293
2021 DC	WAS	MLB	28	3	3	0	14	11	56.7	56	8	3.5	7.8	49	43.6%	.293

Comparables: Zach Davies, Joe Musgrove, Brett Anderson

Sometimes inaction is the best action. The Nationals, in the simpler times of February 2020, entered with a fifth-starter conundrum: Ross, Voth or Fedde. The latter two ended up getting starts throughout the season, while Ross did not—not because he lost the battle or suffered an injury, but because he opted out from the season over COVID-19-related concerns. Ross, who recovered from Tommy John to plug the gap filled by Scherzer's back-related absences in 2019 (most famously during the World Series), figures to return in 2021. Given how Voth and Fedde pitched, the Nationals would be justified to prioritize him in their rotation pecking order.

YEAR	TEAM	LVL	AGE	WHIP	ERA	DRA-	WARP	MPH	FB%	WHF	CSP
2018	NAT	ROK	25	0.50	0.00						
2018	SYR	AAA	25	1.37	3.09	96	0.1				
2018	WAS	MLB	25	1.31	5.06	158	-0.3	94.6	56.0%	17.0%	
2019	FRE	AAA	26	1.40	4.28	96	0.8				
2019	WAS	MLB	26	1.67	5.48	130	-0.5	95.8	62.8%	23.6%	
2021 FS	WAS	MLB	28	1.38	4.64	104	1.1	95.7	62.2%	22.9%	45.3%
2021 DC	WAS	MLB	28	1.38	4.64	104	0.4	95.7	62.2%	22.9%	45.3%

Washington Nationals 2021

Jackson Rutledge   RHP
Born: 04/01/99   Age: 22   Bats: R   Throws: R
Height: 6'8"   Weight: 250   Origin: Round 1, 2019 Draft (#17 overall)

YEAR	TEAM	LVL	AGE	W	L	SV	G	GS	IP	H	HR	BB/9	K/9	K	GB%	BABIP
2019	NAT	ROK	20	0	0	0	1	1	1	4	0	9.0	18.0	2	80.0%	.800
2019	AUB	SS	20	0	0	0	3	3	9	4	2	3.0	6.0	6	41.7%	.091
2019	HAG	LO-A	20	2	0	0	6	6	27^1	14	0	3.6	10.2	31	44.4%	.222
2021 FS	*WAS*	*MLB*	*22*	*2*	*3*	*0*	*57*	*0*	*50*	*47*	*8*	*5.6*	*8.0*	*44*	*40.5%*	*.280*

Comparables: Parker Markel, Mat Latos, Reynaldo López

"What if Aaron Judge but a pitcher?" That's what the scientists on the Nationals apparently are trying to answer with Rutledge. A behemoth of a human at 6-foot-8 and 260 pounds, the righty towers over his peers both in size and stuff: He throws 96-100 mph with ease and pairs that with a plus-plus slider, an above-average curveball and a changeup that is still developing but is a viable fourth pitch. It's terrifying to think about what he could do in relief, and that may be his destiny, as his control is very much a work in progress and his durability is an open question. Does that sound like Dellin Betances to anybody else?

YEAR	TEAM	LVL	AGE	WHIP	ERA	DRA-	WARP	MPH	FB%	WHF	CSP
2019	NAT	ROK	20	5.00	27.00						
2019	AUB	SS	20	0.78	3.00	73	0.2				
2019	HAG	LO-A	20	0.91	2.30	70	0.6				
2021 FS	*WAS*	*MLB*	*22*	*1.57*	*5.36*	*118*	*-0.3*				

Stephen Strasburg RHP

Born: 07/20/88 Age: 32 Bats: R Throws: R
Height: 6'5" Weight: 235 Origin: Round 1, 2009 Draft (#1 overall)

YEAR	TEAM	LVL	AGE	W	L	SV	G	GS	IP	H	HR	BB/9	K/9	K	GB%	BABIP
2018	FBG	HI-A	29	0	1	0	2	2	9	7	1	1.0	12.0	12	50.0%	.261
2018	WAS	MLB	29	10	7	0	22	22	130	118	18	2.6	10.8	156	43.9%	.310
2019	WAS	MLB	30	18	6	0	33	33	209	161	24	2.4	10.8	251	50.4%	.276
2020	WAS	MLB	31	0	1	0	2	2	5	8	1	1.8	3.6	2	35.0%	.368
2021 FS	WAS	MLB	32	10	7	0	26	26	150	131	18	2.6	9.6	159	46.8%	.288
2021 DC	WAS	MLB	32	10	7	0	25	25	145	126	17	2.6	9.6	154	46.8%	.288

Comparables: Jacob deGrom, Clayton Kershaw, Jake Peavy

Strasburg didn't get a real opportunity to follow up on his brilliant postseason efforts from 2019. Instead, injury shortened his truncated season, limiting him to five innings over two appearances before he succumbed to carpal tunnel surgery. He's already retooled once in his career—from fire-thrower to a changeup/curveball artist—and if past performance is a predictor of future performance, past resilience may be a predictor of future adaptability, even as his age increases and velo declines. In other words, the Nationals shouldn't yet fret about the $245 million contract they handed him last winter.

YEAR	TEAM	LVL	AGE	WHIP	ERA	DRA-	WARP	MPH	FB%	WHF	CSP
2018	FBG	HI-A	29	0.89	1.00	61	0.3				
2018	WAS	MLB	29	1.20	3.74	66	3.5	97.1	52.0%	28.0%	
2019	WAS	MLB	30	1.04	3.32	43	8.3	95.6	48.3%	30.7%	
2020	WAS	MLB	31	1.80	10.80	117	0.0	93.2	45.8%	26.3%	
2021 FS	WAS	MLB	32	1.16	3.27	78	3.3	95.9	49.1%	29.9%	45.3%
2021 DC	WAS	MLB	32	1.16	3.27	78	3.1	95.9	49.1%	29.9%	45.3%

Washington Nationals 2021

Austen Williams RHP
Born: 12/19/92 Age: 28 Bats: R Throws: R
Height: 6'3" Weight: 220 Origin: Round 6, 2014 Draft (#184 overall)

YEAR	TEAM	LVL	AGE	W	L	SV	G	GS	IP	H	HR	BB/9	K/9	K	GB%	BABIP
2018	HBG	AA	25	3	3	1	24	2	51^2	34	0	2.3	12.0	69	51.2%	.286
2018	SYR	AAA	25	0	0	1	8	0	16^1	6	0	2.2	11.0	20	58.8%	.176
2018	WAS	MLB	25	0	1	0	10	0	9^2	10	5	5.6	7.4	8	20.0%	.208
2019	HBG	AA	26	0	1	0	5	0	5^1	8	0	5.1	11.8	7	33.3%	.500
2019	WAS	MLB	26	0	0	0	2	0	0^1	5	2	27.0	27.0	1	40.0%	1.000
2021 FS	*WAS*	*MLB*	*28*	*2*	*2*	*0*	*57*	*0*	*50*	*46*	*7*	*3.5*	*8.7*	*48*	*40.6%*	*.284*

Comparables: Kevin McGowan, Erick Fedde, Matt Purke

Williams was unseen in 2020 and will remain so in '21 after undergoing Tommy John surgery in the summer. He's got just 12 MLB appearances to his name and probably won't pitch again until he's 29, if he does at all.

YEAR	TEAM	LVL	AGE	WHIP	ERA	DRA-	WARP	MPH	FB%	WHF	CSP
2018	HBG	AA	25	0.91	1.39	52	1.5				
2018	SYR	AAA	25	0.61	0.55	52	0.5				
2018	WAS	MLB	25	1.66	5.59	135	-0.1	95.7	53.4%	31.2%	
2019	HBG	AA	26	2.06	10.12	139	-0.1				
2019	WAS	MLB	26	18.00	162.00	95	0.0	93.1	37.9%	33.3%	
2021 FS	*WAS*	*MLB*	*28*	*1.30*	*4.09*	*94*	*0.4*	*95.1*	*49.6%*	*31.8%*	*37.2%*

Nationals Prospects

The State of the System:
Flags fly forever, but that flag is a bit further in the rear view mirror now, and objects ahead aren't as close as they appear.

The Top Ten:

1
Cade Cavalli   RHP   OFP: 60   ETA: 2023
Born: 08/14/98   Age: 22   Bats: R   Throws: R   Height: 6'4"   Weight: 226
Origin: Round 1, 2020 Draft (#22 overall)

The Report: The 2020 draft, for obvious reasons, was one of the most difficult ever to evaluate talent. From small sample sizes to no sample size in some cases, there would be risk no matter what strategy an org employed. The Nationals have been known to roll the dice in recent years when it comes to their first round selections, and rather than play it safe with the added uncertainty in 2020, they pressed on the gas once again with Cavalli. The boxy right hander brings the heat with easy mechanics that make his high-90s fastball look effortless. However, injuries have prevented him from pitching for long stretches, with his summer on the Collegiate National Team and superb spring giving glimpses of the elite stuff he brings to the mound. A nasty breaking ball that can be located in the zone or as a swing-and-miss chase pitch. It complements the heater well, as does a developing changeup.

Development Track: It's all about proving his case as a starter. Can he hold up over the course of a full season? And if not, how quickly is he moved as a reliever where his electric stuff could bolster an often suspect Nats bullpen? The health and reliever risks are real. On the other hand, if his most recent history is indicative of the true potential then you put aside those worries until they're actualized.

Variance: Very High. The difference between a top-half-of-the-rotation guy and high-leverage reliever is a significant gap. Both good on their own, with history suggesting the likelier scenario is the one with less stress on the arm.

J.P. Breen's Fantasy Take: While the value differential between a frontline starter and a high-leverage reliever is massive in real-life baseball, it's much smaller in fantasy. Dominant, high-strikeout relievers—whether they are amassing saves are not—have a home in today's fantasy environment. Unlike many of the potential high-leverage relief prospects that we've covered throughout these Top Ten lists, though, Cavalli has a chance to be an impact starter. The health risks keep him outside the top-200 dynasty prospects, but he's a top-25 guy in supplemental drafts this winter.

2. Jackson Rutledge   RHP   OFP: 60   ETA: Late 2022/2023
Born: 04/01/99   Age: 22   Bats: R   Throws: R   Height: 6'8"   Weight: 250
Origin: Round 1, 2019 Draft (#17 overall)

The Report: Out of the gate, the 2019 first rounder hit the ground running, making it to Low-A Hagerstown after short stints in the Gulf Coast and New York-Penn Leagues. Rutledge pitched well with the Suns over six starts, compiling a 2.30 ERA and 31 strikeouts against 11 walks in 27 ⅓ innings. This past year, Rutledge worked on improving his mechanics to boost his command. His fastball—a plus-plus offering—can get as high as 99 with life up in the zone that makes it a swing-and-miss pitch on its own. Backing the heater is a mid-to-upper-80s slider that can also miss bats due to its late break.

Development Track: The slider is clearly his best secondary, so Rutledge worked on his curveball and changeup this past year with positive results. Honing his command and the development of a second go-to offspeed pitch will dictate Rutledge's time table and ultimate major league role, but there's a lot to like here if everything comes together.

Variance: High. The reports from the alternate site are encouraging, but not enough to lower the variance quite yet. Even though he is athletic on the mound, being 6-foot-8 can be worrisome from a mechanical and injury standpoint. More innings on the bump can alleviate that to some degree. There is also high-leverage reliever possibility with his fastball/slider combination if all else fails. But we're not close to that outcome yet.

J.P. Breen's Fantasy Take: Rutledge was one of my favorite pitchers from the 2019 draft class, so I understand that I'm higher on him than most dynasty analysts. Still, he's a potential No. 2 starter and has shown the ability to throw strikes—though maybe not good strikes yet. I'll take the alternate site improvement stories with a grain of salt, as I have all offseason, but I like high-upside arms who have a safe floor of being a potentially elite reliever. Rutledge is flirting with being a top-100 dynasty prospect.

3. Drew Mendoza   3B   OFP: 50   ETA: 2023
Born: 10/10/97   Age: 23   Bats: L   Throws: R   Height: 6'5"   Weight: 230
Origin: Round 3, 2019 Draft (#94 overall)

The Report: A graduate of Florida State with a Masters degree in three-true-outcomes, Mendoza is still a work in progress when it comes to just about every aspect of his game. He's always shown the potential for hitting the ball hard and over the fence, and over time he's tried everything from opening his stance to closing off, tinkering with hand locations, all in an effort to become a more complete hitter. An admirable quest, to say the least. He was fine as a third baseman in college with a short throwing motion, but he's a big man with limited range and the Nats seem content moving him over to first base without delay.

Development Track: The experimentation continued with reports from camp that he was working to be more aggressive in his approach, not letting too many pitches go by that he falls behind in the count. The fact he has shown an openness to work through so many ideas to better himself is a definite plus.

Variance: High. If he doesn't hit enough, if the TTO becomes two or less outcomes, there isn't much else there. Then again, something like .250/.350/.450 is assuredly possible.

J.P. Breen's Fantasy Take: A three-true-outcome profile at first base is rarely an impact profile. The .250/.350/.450 slash line mentioned above is basically what Christian Walker posted in 2019, which is usable but nothing special. Mendoza has to produce elite power numbers to become a Max Muncy or Matt Olson, who are both posting slugging percentages between .510 and .500. Scouting reports suggest that Mendoza has that kind of raw power, but we're nowhere close to seeing him tap into it in games. I don't have him in my personal top-400 dynasty prospects.

4 Tim Cate   LHP   OFP: 50   ETA: Late 2021/Early 2022
Born: 09/30/97   Age: 23   Bats: L   Throws: L   Height: 6'0"   Weight: 185
Origin: Round 2, 2018 Draft (#65 overall)

The Report: Cate had some first-round buzz going into his junior season, due to his very pretty, and very plus curveball. His velocity bounced around early in the season and he was eventually shut down until tourney time, where he came back as a reliever. A possibly balky arm has never scared off the Nats, and Cate tossed more than 140 innings in his first full pro season in 2019. The curve remained far at the head of the arsenal, but there was enough command and cut on the fastball—usually a tick or two either side of 90—to keep righties off the barrel. The profile was on the backend starter side with the fringe fastball and change setting up the hook as a potential out pitch.

Development Track: Cate added a tick or two on the fastball as the alternate site and there were positive change-up developments as well. That bumps the floor as long as the durability issues stay in his rear view mirror. Cate would have started 2020 in Double-A, and may still end up in Harrisburg to open 2021, but I'd also expect him to be in play for major league starts at some point next season as needed. And speaking of durability issues, the Nats rotation has had their fair share recently, so slots might open up.

Variance: Medium. Cate was used heavily at UConn, and his arm paid the price for it. It hasn't lingered as an issue in the pros, but it will be in the back of my mind. Everything else in the profile looks like a fairly safe backend starter. But we will get our one, "also, he's a pitcher" for the year here.

Washington Nationals 2021

J.P. Breen's Fantasy Take: Potential back-end starters who logged a crap ton of innings in college aren't my jam. Cate might be a waiver-wire pickup in deep leagues if he reaches the majors and gets a few starts in 2021, but he'll struggle to carve out a role that makes him fantasy relevant on a yearly basis.

5. Yasel Antuna   SS   OFP: 55   ETA: 2023
Born: 10/26/99   Age: 21   Bats: S   Throws: R   Height: 6'0"   Weight: 170
Origin: International Free Agent, 2016

The Report: Our Antuna report is basically stuck in time at this point. He had Tommy John surgery late in 2018, and missed all but a small handful of GCL rehab games in 2019. Dating back to 2018, he showed wide-ranging potential with very little of it actualized yet. He flashed above-average potential on both hit and power, but wasn't getting them into games as he got eaten alive by full-season pitching. His defense at shortstop was inconsistent, and we've never been sure where he was going to land on the infield.

Development Track: We got very strong positive feedback on Antuna's offensive growth at the alternate site and fall instructs. The Nationals weren't in the alternate site share, so take it with appropriate salt, but the system is so weak that it pushed him up substantially anyway. If he comes out and hits at a full-season level in 2021, there isn't exactly a ton standing in his way from the top of the system.

Variance: Extreme. He still hasn't hit in games above complex ball yet.

J.P. Breen's Fantasy Take: Antuna is one for your watch lists, as he has the potential skills to be a corner- or middle-infield depth piece in most dynasty formats. Still, we haven't seen substantive at-bats from him since 2018. And even then, it wasn't pretty.

6. Cole Henry   RHP   OFP: 50   ETA: 2023
Born: 07/15/99   Age: 21   Bats: R   Throws: R   Height: 6'4"   Weight: 211
Origin: Round 2, 2020 Draft (#55 overall)

The Report: As a high school senior, Henry was well known for his projectable body and big arm. He was mentioned as a possible early Day 2 pick. With a solid commitment to LSU, he went to college and worked on the glaring issue that plagued his prep days: An out-of-control delivery that led to bouts of erratic performances. Positive strides were clearly made as soon as he stepped on campus, especially quieting a violent head whack. It showed as a freshman and really took off during his short draft-eligible sophomore spring. His mid-90s fastball was located to both sides of the plate, and he improved the command of his curveball and changeup both in and out of the zone.

Development Track: Nobody wants to leave the table when you've got a hot hand, and Henry was among those in 2020 who didn't want their streak to end. As hard as he worked on his delivery and improving his changeup, you hope to see that diligence keep pace as he settles in with the Nationals' system. There is still some room for growth and he's yet to pitch a full season, and with that comes questions of the glass half-full or half-empty variety. Can he sustain it? Or is there more beneath the surface that is still untapped?

Variance: Medium. It's easy to fall in love with the most recent game action. The flags remain and will continue to exist until proven otherwise.

J.P. Breen's Fantasy Take: Henry seems to have more upside than his OFP would indicate, due to his impressive pre-COVID-19 showing at LSU, but the fact that he's, at best, a non-frontline pitching prospect keeps him comfortably outside the purview of most dynasty leagues. If he gets hot in 2021 and looks to move quickly as a usable No. 4 starter, he might be worth an add in deeper leagues. Keep him on your watch list for now.

7. Matt Cronin LHP   OFP: 50   ETA: 2021
Born: 09/20/97   Age: 23   Bats: L   Throws: L   Height: 6'2"   Weight: 195
Origin: Round 4, 2019 Draft (#123 overall)

The Report: After being selected in the 2019 draft, Cronin quickly made the jump to Low-A Hagerstown and dominated. Over 22 relief innings, the lefty fanned 41 against 11 walks with a 0.82 ERA. Cronin's explosive fastball sits 93-96 and features late hop that plays well up in the zone. His curveball, mid-70s, is a wipeout offering with a high spin rate, which garners plenty of whiffs. He commands both pitches well. The delivery is quite aggressive and requires a lot of effort but it hasn't been an issue so far, as hitters have trouble timing it up and picking up pitches. Cronin will be a quick mover impacting the big league club in the back end of games sooner than later.

Development Track: As mentioned above, Cronin should move really fast. He won't need a lot of innings at each stop to prove that his stuff is lethal and will continue to garner whiffs as he progresses.

Variance: Low. There isn't much to worry about here, but the upside is also limited to late-inning pen work. One could be concerned about the delivery but so far it's been repeatable and durable for him.

J.P. Breen's Fantasy Take: As I've mentioned often in these blurbs, quality relievers are valued more in fantasy than they've ever been. Rightfully so. Still, they're not worth rostering as prospects. There are too many quality non-closing relievers available in the majors to be worried about that.

8. Andry Lara   OFP: 50   ETA: 2025
Born: 01/06/03   Age: 18   Bats: R   Throws: R   Height: 6'4"   Weight: 180
Origin: International Free Agent, 2019

The Report: Lara has yet to make his official pro debut. However, he had a positive 2020 while training stateside. He has a slow and deliberate windup with easy actions that he repeats. Lara has good arm speed which generates his low-to-mid-90s fastball. He already spins his curveball well and is developing a changeup. The right-hander controls the zone and has a sturdy frame with long limbs. Lara is a quick learner and advanced in a lot of areas for a teenager.

Development Track: Lara was stateside for most of 2020, as returning home to Venezuela became difficult during the pandemic. So traditional thinking would have Lara competing in the complex leagues and get more experience against opposing hitters before sending him to an affiliate. Check back in a year, or two.

Variance: Extreme. Lara hasn't thrown in an official game yet, and likely has another season of extended and complex-level ball ahead of him. There's a lot of ways this profile can go in the next couple years, both positive and negative.

J.P. Breen's Fantasy Take: Dynasty owners can't afford to wait on intriguing J2 bats, but they can absolutely afford to be patient with intriguing J2 arms. Don't worry about Lara until he's producing in full-season ball, unless the stuff really becomes special.

9. Sammy Infante   OFP: 50   ETA: 2024
Born: 06/22/01   Age: 20   Bats: R   Throws: R   Height: 6'1"   Weight: 185
Origin: Round 2, 2020 Draft (#71 overall)

The Report: Not the kind of player who would normally be featured in many top ten lists, and yet, here we are. Infante was a surprise over-slot selection when it was believed he would attend The U, where he could get some additional seasoning and return as a draft-eligible sophomore in 2022. The Nats are a clear believer in the bat, which does have some alluring qualities to it. He tracks the ball well and keeps his body in sync with an uphill swing that can be used to get to his power. Listed as a shortstop, it's believed he'll eventually move off the position, though reports from the org suggest he'll start there and see what happens.

Development Track: The minor league realignment to erase short season affiliates likely puts Infante on track to start in extended spring training or the rookie level Gulf Coast League, depending on whenever the minors (hopefully) get going in 2021. There are some building blocks in his foundation, more on the hitting side, with the rest of his game needing all the nurturing he can get.

Variance: Extreme. Too many unknowns to have a clue which direction it goes.

J.P. Breen's Fantasy Take: With more than a few question marks, Infante is best avoided in dynasty leagues. He's unlikely to see full-season ball in 2021, and he's someone who has shown significant contact issues in the past—and that's without the lighttower power potential that we'd need to see to make him worth rostering in dynasty.

10. Mason Denaburg   RHP   OFP: 50   ETA: 2023/2024
Born: 08/08/99   Age: 21   Bats: R   Throws: R   Height: 6'4"   Weight: 195
Origin: Round 1, 2018 Draft (#27 overall)

The Report: Since before the 2018 draft, Denaburg has been plagued by injuries. Thus far in his professional career he has been able to complete only 20 1/3 innings in the Gulf Coast League in 2019, pitching to a 7.52 ERA with 19 strikeouts against 14 walks. So there's plenty of trepidation with how his career has begun. However, Denaburg is healthy again and pitching in live situations. Before the injuries, Denaburg showed promise with above-average command, offering a mid-90s fastball, sluvry curveball and developing changeup.

Development Track: With the injuries, Denaburg hasn't had time to develop pitches or build up his endurance for a full season. If he can stay healthy, 2021 will be a crucial year developmentally for the right-hander to understand where he needs to improve. Keep a long term outlook here.

Variance: High. Although reportedly healthy, Denaburg will need to demonstrate that health in games in 2021. Until the ledger has more innings the variance will remain.

J.P. Breen's Fantasy Take: A potential back-end starter with a significant injury history? At No. 10? Yikes, at least the Nats have a fun major-league squad!

The Prospects You Meet Outside The Top Ten

Prospects to dream on a little

Jeremy De La Rosa   OF   Born: 01/16/02   Age: 19   Bats: L   Throws: L   Height: 5'11"   Weight: 160   Origin: International Free Agent, 2018

Signed for $300,000 by the Nats in July 2019, de la Rosa's profile is highlighted by plus bat speed and barrel control from the left side of the plate. The bat stays through the zone a long time, which helps him drive the ball to all fields, and the power might end up a little above-average. He will likely end up being an average defender in left so the bat will need to reach close to full potential. de la Rosa will be entering his age-19 season in 2021 and his second stint stateside. Long way to go but there's above-average upside.

Roismar Quintana   OF   Born: 02/06/03   Age: 18   Bats: R   Throws: R   Height: 6'1"   Weight: 175   Origin: International Free Agent, 2019

Signed for $820,000 out of last year's J2 class, Quintana offers potential upside both offensively and defensively. The right-hander has a good feel for the barrel and plus bat speed, showcasing burgeoning power. Quintana has a chance to stick in center with his present defensive aptitude, but may eventually be moved to left as he fills out his already quite physical frame. There isn't a tool that will wow you. However, the 18-year-old has a broad base of tools that are intriguing.

MLB bats, but less upside than you'd like

Jackson Cluff   SS   Born: 12/03/96   Age: 24   Bats: L   Throws: R   Height: 6'0"   Weight: 185   Origin: Round 6, 2019 Draft (#183 overall)

Although an older prospect because he spent two years on a mission while attending Brigham Young University, Ciuff possesses plus defensive skills at shortstop with his range, actions, and arm all grading out as above-average. Seen as a possible super-utility infielder, Cluff is also an above-average to plus runner, swiping 11 bags in 63 games with Low-A Hagerstown in 2019. The lefty in the box has a quick stroke with some pull side pop but is working to stay inside the ball more and lay off pitches out of the zone.

Top Talents 25 and Under (as of 4/1/2021):

1. Juan Soto, OF
2. Victor Robles, OF
3. Carter Kieboom, 3B
4. Luis García, 2B/SS
5. Cade Cavalli, RHP
6. Jackson Rutledge, RHP
7. Drew Mendoza, 3B/1B
8. Tim Cate, LHP
9. Yasel Antuna, IF
10. Cole Henry, RHP

If you have a young star as good as Juan Soto, your farm system being on a downswing hurts a lot less. Soto turned 22 during the World Series. He was, by nearly any metric, one of the best hitters in baseball in 2020. And that's his true talent.

Victor Robles's offensive output has been trending down for three seasons now, which isn't what you want from a young potential star. His average exit velocity dipped to 82.2 mph in 2020, the absolute worst in MLB. Robles never had a lot of power in his profile, but he should have more than that. At least he's still stellar in center field.

Carter Kieboom's hit tool—which we projected as high as plus as a prospect—has deserted him in the majors so far. His power deserted him in 2020 as well, with just one double and zero homers in 122 plate appearances, but he still put up an 86 DRC+ and 0.5 WARP. I don't know where this is going, but it's worth keeping in mind that as bad as he's been in the majors, it's been over just 165 plate appearances in two seasons, and at this time last year he'd been a Top 20 prospect for two years running.

Luis García came up just three months after his 20th birthday, coming off an age-19 season where he struggled mightily at Double-A. He certainly wasn't good—he racked up a -1.3 WARP in only 139 plate appearances—but he still probably did better than you'd expect someone who slashed .257/.280/.337 at Double-A last year to do. Were he a prospect, he might've even made the Top 101.

Part 3: Featured Articles

Nationals All-Time Top 10 Players

by Rob Mains

POSITION PLAYERS

GARY CARTER, C (1974-1984, 1992)
Carter led the league in games caught every year from 1976 to 1982, catching 146 or more in all but two of them (one of those a strike year). Despite a withering workload at the game's toughest position, he had an .804 OPS those seasons, 22 percent above the league, averaging 27 homers and 91 RBI per year. He won three Gold Gloves and received MVP votes in five of his Expos seasons, drove in 100 runs twice, and was a fan favorite.

RYAN ZIMMERMAN, 1B/3B (2005-2019)
The franchise record-holder for home runs with 270 and RBI with 1,015, Zimmerman played in every Nationals season until he opted out of 2020. His walk-off homer in the nationally-televised first game at Nationals Park in 2008 is one of the most famous hits in franchise history. Injuries limited him to only seven full seasons with the club, but he averaged 27 homers and 96 RBI in those years, hitting .287/.354/.495. He'll be back for possibly his final year in 2021.

TIM WALLACH, 3B (1980-1992)
No player in franchise history appeared in more games than Wallach's 1,767. He was durable, playing 150 or more games in ten of the eleven seasons between 1982 and 1992, averaging 323 doubles and 18 homers per season. He was an outstanding defender, winning three Gold Gloves. When he drove in 123 runs in 1987, he set a franchise record that stood for a dozen seasons.

ANTHONY RENDON, 3B (2013-2019)

He was one of the National League's best hitters during his Nationals tenure, hitting .290/.369/.490. He hit 20-plus homers in each of his five full seasons, hit more than 40 doubles three times (leading the league twice), and scored 100 runs and drove in 100 twice. During the team's 17-game drive to the World Championship in 2019, he hit .328/.413/.590 with three homers and 15 RBI.

RUSTY STAUB, OF (1969-1971, 1979)

"Le Grand Orange," wildly popular with Expos fans, had only three full years in Montreal but was the team's first star. Yet another great player who was driven out of Houston by Harry Walker, Staub was traded to the Expos for veterans Donn Clendenon and Jesus Alou. Clendenon refused to play for the racist Walker, so the Astros had to accept substitutes. Staub was Montreal's best player in each of its first three seasons, playing all but six of the team's games. He hit .296/.404/.501 with an average of 26 homers and 90 RBI per year for an expansion team that lost 289 games.

ANDRE DAWSON, OF (1976-1986)

The 1977 Rookie of the Year won four Gold Gloves for his play in center field. When his aching knees forced a move to right field, he won two more. But he's remembered mostly for his bat, as he hit .280/.326/.476 as an Expo, third on the all-time franchise list for homers, RBI, and runs, second for triples, and fourth for doubles. He had an above-average OPS every year with the club. The artificial turf at Stade Olympique led only the park's dimensions itself in the extent to which it damaged him—he hit .267/.322/.448 with 95 home runs at home, .292/.329/.503 with 130 home runs on the road.

TIM RAINES, OF (1979-1990)

Kid, Hawk, and Rock were the three best Expos. Raines, arguably the best leadoff hitter ever not named Rickey Henderson, averaged 63 stolen bases in ten years as an Expos regular, leading the league from 1981 to 1984 with totals of 71, 78, 90, and 75. He had outstanding on-base skills, with an on-base percentage of .391, and had a .437 slugging percentage thanks to 30-odd doubles and a dozen or so homers per year. He scored 100 runs four times, leading the league twice. Legendary moment: In 1987, having missed spring training and the first month of a season due to one of baseball's sado-masochistic rules of free agency during collusion, walked into his first game cold and hit a game-winning, 10th-inning grand slam.

LARRY WALKER, OF (1989-1994)

He achieved greater fame after signing a free-agent contract with the Rockies, but Walker averaged 28 doubles, 20 homers, and 19 stolen bases in his five full seasons with Montreal, winning two Gold Gloves with his outstanding play in right field. In his best year, he hit .322/.394/.587 with a league-leading 44 doubles when the 1994 strike ended his last Expos season. He's the best native Canadian to have played for the Expos.

VLADIMIR GUERRERO, OF (1996-2003)
The best of the end-of-the-line Expos, Guerrero starred for teams that had only two winning seasons—both of them four games over .500—in his years as a regular. He played almost every game and was the franchise's best hitter, with a .323 batting average, .588 slugging percentage, and .978 OPS. He twice had 200 hits, averaged 39 homers and 116 RBI in his five full years, and stole as many as 40 bases in a season. Memorable for his cannon arm and his ability to drive any pitch, even the occasional one that bounced in front of the plate.

BRYCE HARPER, OF (2012-2018)
Brash, controversial, and with the talent to match, Harper had All-Star game, Rookie of the Year, and MVP votes while still a teenager. His MVP season in 2015, featuring 42 homers and a 1.109 OPS, is the most dominant post-Steroid Era season in the National League. His .900 OPS with Washington is the highest in Nationals history and second to Guerrero for the franchise. The only thing missing was consistency anywhere near that level, but very few players in history have been able to get there or stay there.

PITCHERS

STEVE ROGERS, RHP (1973-1985)
From 1973 to 1978 he pitched for Expos teams that never had a winning record, leading the league in losses twice despite a 3.15 ERA that was 20 percent better than average. Pitching for better clubs from 1979 to 1983, his 2.97 ERA was similarly better-than-average but he won over 60 percent of his decisions, averaging 15-10, with better support. His high workload—he averaged 250 innings pitched per year from 1974 to 1983—eventually caused his shoulder to go, but he's the franchise leader, by far, in starts, innings, and wins.

BRYN SMITH, RHP (1981-1989)
Smith was a reliever his first full year in the league, appearing in 47 games in 1982. He was a swingman the next year and joined the rotation in 1984. In his nine years in the rotation, he was 72-56 with a 3.33 ERA. He walked only six percent of the batters he faced and ranks fifth in franchise history at suppressing walks. In 1985, 1987, and 1989 he walked fewer than two batters per nine innings, leadsing the league with just 1.5 walks per nine in 1988.

DENNIS MARTINEZ, RHP (1986-1993)

He was 32 and seemed washed up, in part due to alcoholism, when the Expos acquired him for a player to be named later in 1986. He started 15 games for the club that year and 22 the next then became its most reliable starter, averaging 33 starts, 228 innings, and a 14-10 record with a 2.92 ERA between 1988 and 1993. He won the ERA crown in 1991 with a 2.39 mark, and his 3.06 with the team is second in franchise history. The first Nicaraguan in the majors pitched a perfect game in 1991—and he recovered from his drinking problem too.

PEDRO MARTÍNEZ, RHP (1994-1997)

OK, maybe trading the best pitcher of his era to Boston wasn't a great idea, but getting him from the Dodgers may have saved his arm from being shredded by that club's (read: Tommy Lasorda's) propensity for overuse. He won the Cy Young Award his last year with the Expos, going 17-8 with a 1.90 ERA and 305 strikeouts in 241 1/3 innings during the Steroid Era. His 3.06 ERA is the fifth-lowest in franchise history and his 26 percent strikeout rate is the highest in Expos history.

JAVIER VÁZQUEZ, RHP (1998-2003)

He was a workhorse for the Expos, pitching an average of 205 innings per year over 32 stars with the club. His Steroid Era 4.16 ERA was seven percent better than average during his time with the club. His best season was 2001, when he was 16-11 with 3.42 ERA for a team that went 68-94.

LIVÁN HERNÁNDEZ, RHP (2003-2006, 2009-2011)

In his first stint with the club, split between Montreal and Washington, he led the league in innings pitched three times and starts twice, the best pitcher on the club until he was traded in 2006. In his second stint, playing for losing clubs each year, he was less successful. He ranks sixth in team history with 1,317 innings and had a better-than-average 3.98 ERA.

JORDAN ZIMMERMANN, RHP (2009-2015)

He led the league with 19 wins in 2013 and 33 starts in 2015. His Nationals years featured a 70-50 record and 3.32 ERA. In 2014, he pitched a no-hitter and is remembered for one of the most painful games in franchise history. He was lifted by Matt Williams with two outs in the ninth inning of the second game of the NLDS, leading 1-0, after issuing a bases-empty walk. The reliever allowed a single and game-tying double in a game the Nationals lost in 18 innings.

STEPHEN STRASBURG, RHP (2010-2020)

The Nationals had the first pick in the 2010 and 2011 drafts—losing 196 games over two years gets you that—and with Strasburg in 2010 and Harper in 2011 they got two of the most-hyped draftees in history. Strasburg starts were must-see events for the woeful Nats, with the rookie striking out 34 percent of the batters he faced, right up until he tore his ulnar collateral ligament in August. He came back in 2012 but management shut him down in early September, very possibly costing them a deep postseason run. He's battled injuries since but led the league in innings and wins in 2019. He leads the franchise in career strikeouts and despite his injuries is second to Rogers with 241 starts.

GIO GONZALEZ, LHP (2012-2018)

Drafted by the White Sox, he was traded to the Phillies, back to the White Sox, and to the A's before the Nationals got him. His first season in Washington was his best: He had a league-leading 21 wins and only 8 losses, 2.89 ERA, 199 1/3 innings, had the most strikeouts and fewest homers allowed per nine innings in the league. His last full year, 2017, was strong as well: 15-9, with a 2.96 ERA, fifth in the league. He led the team in starts and innings while with the club.

MAX SCHERZER, RHP (2015-2020)

Excluding the shortened 2020 season, Scherzer's five seasons with the Nationals have yielded five of the eight highest strikeout totals in team history. He won back-to-back Cy Young Awards in 2016 and 2017, has allowed less than a baserunner per inning, and has a 2.80 ERA with the Nationals, 53 percent better than average, best ever for the team. He's struck out 5.8 batters for every one he's walked; nobody else in team history has a ratio greater than 4.5.

A Taxonomy of 2020 Abnormalities

by Rob Mains

I'm going to start this with a trivia question. Trust me, it's relevant. Don't bother skipping to the end of the article to find the answer, it's not there.

Only five players have appeared in 140 or more games for 16 straight seasons. Who are they?

It's a trivia question starting off an essay, so you know how this works: Whatever you guessed, you're wrong. It's okay. As someone who purchased this book, chances are good that you're an educated baseball fan. But the circumstances behind 2020 force us to abandon, or at least seriously question, some of our favorite patterns and crutches for evaluating the game we love.

We just completed what was undoubtedly the strangest season in MLB history. No fans, geographically limited schedule, universal DH, seven-inning twin bills, runners on second in extra innings, a 16-team postseason, a club playing at a Triple-A stadium. Some of these changes will likely persist (sorry), but we've never had so many tweaks dumped on us all at once, at least not since they figured out how many balls were in a walk.

And the biggest, of course, was the 60-game season. The 19th century was dotted with teams that went bankrupt before the season ended, but the lone season with only 60 scheduled games was 1877. That year there were only six teams, the league rostered a total of 77 players (just 16 more than the 2020 Marlins), and batters called for pitches to be thrown high or low by the pitcher, who was 50 feet away. We can say the 2020 season was easily the shortest ever for recognizable baseball.

As such, it'll stand out. Few abbreviated seasons do. Just about everybody reading this knows the 1994 season ended after Seattle's Randy Johnson struck out Oakland's Ernie Young for the last out of the Mariners-A's game on August 11. The ensuing player strike wiped out the rest of the season and the postseason. Teams played only 112-117 games that year.

And many of you know that a strike in the middle of the 1981 season split the season in two, resulting in the only Division Series until 1995. Teams played only 103-111 games that year, the shortest regular season since 1885.

Those two seasons are memorable. So when we see that nobody drove in 100 runs in 1981, or that Greg Maddux was the only pitcher with 180 or more innings pitched in 1994, we think, "Of course. Strike year."

But we don't remember other short years. You might not recall that the 1994 strike spilled into the next year, chopping 18 games off the 1995 schedule. You might've read that the 1918 season, played during the last pandemic, ended after Labor Day due to the government's World War I "work or fight" order. A strike erased the first week and a half of the 1972 season, but that year's best known as the last time pitchers batted in the American League.

The point is, while we don't remember small changes to the schedule, we remember the big ones. The 1981 mid-season strike. The 1994 season- and Series-ending strike. And, of course, the pandemic-shortened 2020 season. We won't need a reminder why Marcell Ozuna's 18 homers were the fewest to lead the National League in a century. (Literally; Cy Williams led with 15 in 1920.)

Now, about that trivia question. The five players are Hank Aaron, Brooks Robinson, Pete Rose, Ichiro Suzuki, and Johnny Damon. The one nobody gets, of course, is Damon, and a lot of people miss Ichiro, whose last season of 140-plus games came garbed in the red-orange and ocean blue of Miami when he was 42. That's half of what makes it a good question. The other half is the two guys whom many think made the list but didn't. Lou Gehrig? His streak started in the Yankees' 42nd game of the 1925 season and lasted only 13 seasons after that. And everybody assumes Cal Ripken Jr. did it, having played 2,632 straight games over 17 seasons. But one of those 17 seasons was 1994, when the Orioles played only 112 games.

My point? *I just told you* everybody remembers the 1994 strike year, but everybody forgets it fell in the middle of Ripken's streak, separating the first twelve years from the last four. Just because we recall something doesn't mean it's always at the front of our minds.

Nobody is going to forget 2020, and baseball is obviously not the main reason. But there will come a time in the future when you're looking at a player's or a team's record, and there will be baffling numbers there for 2020, and you'll think, "I wonder what happened." (Not to mention the missing line for minor league players.) Just like you forgot that the 1994 strike limited Ripken to 112 games.

Try not to forget it, though. The 2020 season resulted in weird statistical results for several reasons.

There were only 60 games.
I know, duh. But that had impacts beyond counting stats like Ozuna's home run total or Yu Darvish and Shane Bieber leading the majors with eight wins. (I know, pitcher wins, but still.)

The 162-game season is the longest among major North American sports, and that duration gives us a gift. Over the course of a long season, small variations tend to even out. A player who has a ten-game hot streak will probably have a ten-game cold streak. A team that starts the year losing a bunch of close games will probably win a bunch of them. We get regression to the mean. Statistics stabilize.

Consider flipping a coin. Over the long run, we expect it to come up heads about half the time. But the fewer flips, the more variation there'll be. If you flip a coin six times, probability theory tells us you'll get at least two-third heads about 34 percent of the time. Flip it 30 times, your chance of two-thirds heads drops to five percent.

Or, relevant to this case, if you flip a coin 60 times, your chance of getting at least 36 heads—that's 60 percent—is 7.75 percent. Expand the coin-flipping to 162 times, and the chance of getting 60 percent heads drops to 0.73 percent.

In other words, the odds of an outcome that's 20 percent better (or worse) than expected is *more than ten times higher* when you flip your coin 60 times than when you do it 162 times. Call it small sample size, call lack of mean reversion, or call it luck not evening out, 162 is a lot more predictive than 60. You get much more variation over 60 games than over 162. Bieber's 1.63 ERA and 0.87 FIP aren't something we'd see over a full season, and neither is Javier Baéz's .203/.238/.360.

Some players' lines in 2020 look normal. Brian Anderson had an .811 OPS in 2019 and an .810 OPS in 2020. (He probably would have gotten that last point if he'd been given enough time.) But there are many like Bieber and Baéz, some of them from young players still establishing their talent levels. The answer to the question, "What went right or wrong for that guy in 2020?" is most likely "Nothing, it was just a 2020 thing."

Preseason training was abbreviated for hitters.
Every year, spring training drags. Players get tired of it, fans get tired of it, and you sure can tell sportswriters get tired of it. Yes, something to get everyone into shape is necessary, but does it really have to drag on for over a month? Can't we shorten it?

The 2020 season answered in the negative, at least for hitters. Warren Spahn is credited with saying that hitting is timing and pitching is upsetting timing. It appears nobody had his timing down after the abbreviated July summer camp. Through August 9—18 games into the season—MLB batters were hitting .230/.311/.395 with a .275 BABIP. That BABIP, had it held, would have been the lowest since 1968, the Year of the Pitcher. In recent years it's hovered around .300.

It didn't hold. Play returned to more normal levels the rest of the year: .249/.325/.425 with a .297 BABIP starting August 10. But batters whose play concentrated in those first two weeks wound up with ugly lines. Andrew

Washington Nationals 2021

Benintendi went on the injured list with a season-ending rib cage strain on August 11. His final line: .103/.314/.128 in 14 games. Franchy Cordero went on the IL with a hamate bone fracture on August 9 and a .154/.185/.231 line. Even though he came back strong in a late September return, it was too late to repair his full-season numbers.

Preseason training was abbreviated for pitchers.
Every year, spring training drags. Players get tired of it, fans get tired of it ... wait, I already said that. But the abbreviated preseason was tough on pitchers, too. As noted, they had the upper hand coming out of the gate. But then they lost that hand. And then their arms, too.

The 2020 season was spread over 67 days. During those 67 days, 237 pitchers hit the Injured List, compared to 135 in the first 67 days of 2019. A lot of those IL stints, though, were COVID-19-related. Still, over the first 67 days of the 2019 season, there were 72 pitchers on the IL with arm injuries. That figure jumped to 110 in 2020, a 53 percent increase.

There are a number of factors contributing to pitcher arm injuries, ranging from usage to velocity, but it appears that attenuated preseason training played a role. A lot of pitchers had super-short seasons due to arm woes. Corey Kluber, Roberto Osuna, and Shohei Ohtani combined for seven innings, none after August 8. All suffered arm injuries. We'll never know whether they'd have fared better with a longer preseason, but we can guess how they probably feel.

Everybody played.
Rosters were set to expand from 25 to 26 in 2020, so even if we'd had a normal season, we'd have likely seen 2019's record of 1,410 players on MLB rosters broken. But due to the pandemic, rosters started the year at 30 and were cut to only 28. Add multiple COVID-19 absences and the revolving door caused by poor starts by hitters and a rash of pitcher arm injuries, and 1,289 players appeared in MLB games in 2020. The comparable figure over the first 67 days of the 2019 season was 1,109. That 16 percent increase works out to an average of six more players per team in 2020 compared to a similar slice of 2019. A future look back at 2020 rosters will include a lot of unfamiliar names.

Plus became a minus.
In advanced metrics, we adjust batter and pitcher performance for park and league/era variations. A plus sign appended to the end of a measure means that it's adjusted for park and league. It's scaled to an average of 100, with higher figures above average and lower figures below average. (Similarly, a metric with a minus is also park- and league-adjusted and scaled to 100, with lower values better.) Here at BP, our advanced measure of offensive performance is DRC+. Baseball-Reference has OPS+ and FanGraphs has wRC+.

Using park and league adjustments, we can compare Dante Bichette's 1995 Steroid Era season at pre-humidor Coors Field (.340/.364/.620, 40 homers, 128 RBI, MVP runner-up) with Jim Wynn's 1968 Year of the Pitcher season at the cavernous Astrodome (.269/.376/.474, 26 homers, 67 RBI, no MVP votes). It's not close. DRC+, OPS+, and wRC+ all give the nod to Wynn, handily. This is a useful tool. As my Baseball Prospectus colleague Patrick Dubuque tweeted last fall, "Please note that when I ask how you are, I am already adjusting for era."

The 2020 season messes up plus (and minus) stats for two reasons. First, the park adjustment was based on only 30 home games instead of the usual 81. Everything noted above regarding the short season applies, literally doubly, to park effect calculations. DRC+ uses a single-season park factor. OPS+ uses a three-year average and wRC+ five years. The figure for 2020 is suspect.

Second, OPS+ and wRC+ adjust for league: American and National. (DRC+ adjusts for opponent, regardless of league.) While there were two leagues in 2020, they were an artificial construct. To reduce travel, teams played opponents geographically, not based on league. There weren't two leagues, American and National. There were three, Western, Central, and Eastern.

That makes a difference because teams in the same league played in different run-scoring environments. AL teams scored 4.58 runs per game, NL teams 4.71. That's a small difference. But teams in the East scored 0.21 more runs per game (4.95) than teams in the West (4.74), and they both scored a lot more than Central teams (4.25). Adjusting for league misses that difference, so this book will be safe in that regard, but other sources may be distorted somewhat.

Not every game was a "game."
In 2020, the rising tide of strikeouts was finally stemmed. Strikeouts per team per game fell from 8.8 in 2019 to 8.7 in 2020. That marked the first decline after 14 straight annual increases.

In 2020, the rising tide of strikeouts rose higher. Batters struck out in 23.4 percent of plate appearances compared to 23.0 percent in 2019. That marked the 15th straight annual increase.

Both are true statements.

Because of two rule changes—seven-inning doubleheaders and runners on second in extra innings—games in 2020 were unprecedented in their brevity. There were 37.0 plate appearances per game in 2020. The only years with fewer were 1904 and 1906-1909. The average game in 2020 entailed 8.61 innings pitched, the fewest since 1899.

So when you see any per-game stats for 2020, you need to increase them by 3 or 4 percent to get them on equal footing with recent years.

Washington Nationals 2021

Or, better, just ignore them. Last year happened. There were major league games contested between major league teams. But when you're looking at those physical or electronic baseball cards, when you're weaving narratives over why this young player's inevitable rise to stardom fell apart or why that old veteran rekindled his magic, don't linger on the 2020 line. It was just too weird.

Thanks to Lucas Apostoleris for research assistance.

—Rob Mains is an author of Baseball Prospectus.

Tranches of WAR

by Russell A. Carleton

We ask "replacement level" to be a lot of things. Sometimes contradictory things. Sometimes I wonder if we know what it even means anymore. The original idea was that it represented the level of production that a team could expect to get from "freely available talent", including bench players, minor leaguers, and waiver wire pickups. It created a common benchmark to compare everyone to, and for that reason, it represented an advancement well beyond what was available at the time. In fact, it created a language and a framework for evaluating players that was not just better but *entirely* different than what came before it.

But then we started mumbling in that language. The idea behind "wins above replacement" was one part sci-fi episode and one part mathematical exercise. Imagine that a player had disappeared before the season and suddenly, in an alternate timeline, his team would have had to replace him. The distance between him and that replacement line was his value. We need to talk about that alternate timeline.

Without getting too into 2:00 am "deep conversations" with extensive navel-gazing, it's worth thinking about why one player might not be playing, while another might.

- A player might not be playing because he has a short-term injury or his manager believes that he needs a day off.
- A player might not be playing because he has a longer-term injury that requires him to be on the injured list.

There's a difference here between these two situations. In particular, the first one generally *doesn't* involve a compensatory roster move, while the second one does. It's possible, though not guaranteed, that the person who will be replacing the injured/resting player would be the same in either case. That matters. Teams generally carry a spare part for all eight position players on the diamond, although in the era of a four-player bench, those spare parts usually are the backup plan for more than one spot.

Washington Nationals 2021

A couple of years ago, I posed a hypothetical question. Suppose that a team had two players in its system fighting for a fourth outfielder spot. One of them was a league average hitter, but would be worth 20 runs below average if allowed to play center field for a full season. One of them was a perfectly average fielder, but would be 15 runs below average as a hitter, if allowed to play an entire season. Which of the two should the team roster? It's tempting to say the second one, as overall, he is the better player. That misses the point. A league average hitter on the bench isn't just a potential replacement for an injured outfielder. He might also pinch hit for the light-hitting shortstop in a key spot. You keep the average hitter on the roster, even though he isn't a hand-in-glove fit for one specific place on the field, because being a bench player is a different job description than being a long-term fill-in for someone. If you find yourself in need of a longer-term fill-in, you can bring the other guy up from AAA.

When we're determining the value of an everyday player though, if he had disappeared before the season and a team would have had to replace his production, they likely would have done it with a player who was a long-term fill-in type because they would have had to replace a guy who played everyday. Maybe that's the same guy that they would have rostered on their bench anyway, but we don't know. It gets to the query of what we hope to accomplish with WAR. Are we looking for an accurate modeling of reality or are we looking for a common baseline to compare everyone to? Both have their uses, but they are somewhat different questions.

Let's talk about another dichotomy.

- A player might not be playing because he isn't very good and is a bench-level player.
- A player might not be playing because there is another player on the team who has a situational advantage that makes him the better choice today. The classic case of this is a handedness platoon. On another day, he might be a better choice.

When we think about player usage, I think we're still stuck in the model that there are starters and there are scrubs. We have plenty of words for bench players or reserves or backups or utility guys. We do still have the word "platoon" in our collective vocabulary, but in the age of short benches, it's hard to construct one. It's always been hard to construct them. You have to find two players who hit with different hands, have skill sets that complement each other, and probably play the same position. In the era of the short bench, one of them had probably better double as a utility player in some way. Baseball has a two-tiered language geared toward the idea of regulars and reserves. The fact that it was so easy for me to find plenty of synonyms for "a player whose primary function is to come into a game to replace a regular player if he is injured or resting" should tell you something.

I'm always one to look for "unspoken words" in baseball. What is it called when someone is both half of a platoon and the utility infielder? That guy exists sometimes, but he reveals himself in that role—usually by accident. We don't have a word for that, and whenever I find myself saying "we don't have a word for that", I look for new opportunities. What do you call it, further, when the job of being the utility infielder is decentralized across the whole infield with occasional contributions from the left fielder? It's not even a "super-utility" player. What happens when you build your entire roster around the idea that everyone will be expected to be a triple major?

⚾ ⚾ ⚾

I think someone else beat me to this one, and on a grand scale. Platoons work because we know that hitters of the opposite hand to the pitcher get better results than hitters of the same hand, usually to the tune of about 20 points of OBP. If you want to express that in runs, it usually comes out to somewhere around 10 to 12 runs of linear weights value prorated across 650 PA. But hang on a second, now let's say that we have two players who might start today, both of roughly equal merit with the bat. One has a handedness advantage, but is the worse fielder of the two. In that case, as long as his "over the course of a season" projection as a fielder at whatever position you want to slot him into is less than a 10-run drop from the guy he might replace, then he's a better option today.

We're not used to thinking of utility players as bat-first options, who would play below-average defense at three different infield positions. That guy might hook on as a 2B/3B/LF type (Howie Kendrick, come on down!) but teams usually think to themselves that they need as their utility infielder someone who "can handle" shortstop, the toughest of the infield spots to play. If someone can do that *and* hit well, he's probably already starting somewhere, so he's not available as a utility infielder. It's easier for those glove guys to find a job. In a world where the replacement for a shortstop *has to be* the designated utility infielder, that makes sense.

But as we talked about last week, we're living in a different world. The rate at which a replacement for a regular starter turns out to be *another starter* shifting over to cover has gone way up over the last five years. There was always some of it in the game, but this has been a supernova of switcheroos. Now if your second baseman is capable of playing a decent shortstop, that 2B/3B/LF guy can swap in. He's not actually playing shortstop, and maybe the defense suffers from the switch, but if he's got enough of a bat, he might outhit those extra fielding miscues. And in doing so, he is effectively your backup shortstop.

Somewhere along the lines, teams got hip to the idea of multi-positional play from their regulars. I've written before about how you can't just put a player, however athletic, into a new position and expect much at first. The data tell us that. Eventually, players can learn to be multi-positionalists, but it takes time, roughly on the order of two months, before they're OK. But there's a hidden message in there. If you give a player some reps at a new spot, he's a reasonably gifted athlete and somewhat smart and willing to learn, he could probably pick it up enough to get to "good enough," and it doesn't take forever. You just have to be purposeful about it. Maybe you get to the point where you can start to say "he's still below average but we could move him there and get another bat into the lineup, and it's a net win."

Teams have started to build those extra lessons into their player development program. It used to be seen as a mark of weakness to be relegated to "utility player" because that meant that you were a bench player (all those synonyms above come with a side of stigma). Now, it's a way of building a team. If you get a few reps in the minors (where it doesn't count) at a spot, you'll have at least played the spot at game speed before. There are limits to how far you can push that. A slow-footed "he's out in left field because we don't have the DH" guy is never going to play short, but maybe your third baseman can try second base and not look like a total moose out there.

⚾   ⚾   ⚾

Back to WAR. I'd argue that the world of starters and scrubs is slowly disintegrating, for good cause. In the event that a regular starter really does go down with an injury–ostensibly, the alternate universe scenario that WAR is attempting to model–it makes the team a little more resilient to replacing him. And the good news is that you're more likely to be able to replace him with the best of the bench bunch, rather than the third-best guy, because the best guy doesn't have to be an exact positional match for the guy who got hurt. And that's what the manager would want to do. He'd want to replace that long-term production, not with an amalgam of everyone else who played that position, but with the best guy available from his reserves.

Now this is still WAR. We still want to retain the principle that we should be measuring a player, and not his teammates. We need some sort of common baseline, and despite what I just said, we'll still need some sort of amalgam. To construct that, I give to you the idea of the tranche. The word, if you've not heard it before, refers to a piece of a whole that is somehow segmented off. It's often used in finance to talk about layers of a financial instrument.

Here, I want you to consider that there are 30 starters at each of the seven non-battery positions (catchers should have their own WAR, since only a catcher can replace a catcher). We can identify them by playing time, and we can futz around with the definition a little bit if we need to. Next, among those who aren't in that starting pool, we identify the top tranche of the 30 best bench players, which I would again identify by playing time, and then the second and third and fourth and so on. If a player were to disappear, his manager would probably want to take a guy from that top tranche of the bench to replace him. In a world where even the starters can slide around the field, that becomes more feasible.

We can take a look at that top tranche and say "How many of them showed that they are able to play (first, second, etc.)?" and therefore could have directly substituted for the starter? How many of them could have been a direct substitute for our injured player? We don't know whether one of them would be on *a specific* team, but we can say that 40 percent of the time, a manager would have been able to draw from tranche 1 in filling the role, and 35 percent from tranche 2. But on tranche 1, we can also look at how many of those players played a position that could have then shifted and covered for that spot. We'd need some eligibility criteria for all of this (probably a minimum number of games played) but it would just be a matter of multiplication. Shortstop would be harder to fill, and managers would probably be dipping a little further down in the talent pool, and so replacement level would be lower, as it is now.

Doing some quick analysis, I found that the difference in just batting linear weights (haven't even gotten into running or fielding) between tranche 1 and tranche 2 in 2019 was about 6.5 runs, prorated across 650 PA. Between tranche 1 and tranche 3, it's 10.8 runs. The ability to shift those plate appearances up the ladder has some real value.

This part is important. We can also give credit to starters for the positions that they showed an ability to play, even if they didn't play them (this is the guy fully capable of playing center, but who's in a corner because the team already has a good center fielder) because he allows a team to carry a player who hits like a left fielder to functionally be the team's backup center fielder. He facilitates that movement upward among the tranches. We can start to appreciate the difference between a left fielder who would never be able to hack it in center (and the compensatory move that his team would have to make) and the left fielder who could do it, but just didn't have to very often.

Past that, you can continue to use whatever hitting and fielding and running metrics you like to determine a player's value, but when we get down to constructing that baseline, I'd argue we need a better conceptual and mathematical framework. It's going to require some more #GoryMath than we're used to, but I'd argue it's a better conceptualization of the way that MLB actually plays the game in 2020. If…y'know…MLB plays in 2020. If WAR is going to be our flagship statistic among the *acronymati*, then we need to acknowledge that it contains some old and starting-to-be-out-of-date assumptions about the game. We may need to tinker with it. Here's my idea for how.

—Russell A. Carleton *is an author of Baseball Prospectus.*

Secondhand Sport

by Patrick Dubuque

Back before time stopped, I liked to go to thrift stores. Now that I'm older, I rarely ever buy anything—I don't need much in my life, now—but I still enjoy the old familiar circuit: check to see if there are baseball cards to write about, look for board or card games to play with the kids, scan for random ironic jerseys, hit the book section. It takes ten, maybe fifteen minutes. Thrift stores are the antithesis of modern online shopping, because you don't know what they have, and you don't even really know what you want. It's junk, literal junk, stuff other people thought was worthless. That's what makes it great.

In an idealized economy, thrift stores shouldn't exist. Everybody has a living wage, and every product has a durability that exactly matches its desired life; nothing should need to be given away, no one should need to be given to. But then, thrift stores shouldn't work on a customer experience level, either. You wouldn't think an ethos of "let's make everything disorganized and hard to find" would lead to customer satisfaction, but low-budget retailers like TJ Maxx and Ross thrive on this model. People like bargain hunting as much for the hunting as the bargain; it's part of the experience, spending time as if it's a wager. There's a thrill, occasionally, in inefficiency.

In sports, the modern overuse of the word "inefficiency" is a condemnation: It insinuates that there is *an* efficiency, a correct way to be found, and that all other ways are wrong ways. It's prevalent in baseball but hardly contained to it; the lifehack, the Silicon Valley disruption are other examples of productivity creep in our daily lives. Their modern success makes plenty of sense. Maximization of resources, after all, is its own puzzle, and an industry of European board games is founded upon it. It's fun to take a system and optimize it, unravel it like a sudoku puzzle. If there's only one kind of genius, after all, there's no way anyone can fail to appreciate it.

Baseball has been hacking away at these perceived inefficiencies since its inception: platoons, bullpens, farm systems were all installed to extract more out of the tools at hand. But it's been a particular badge of the sabermetric movement, from Ken Phelps and his All-Star Team to Ricardo Rincon and the darlings of *Moneyball*. It's business, but it's also an ethos: the idea that there's treasure among the trash, something we all failed to appreciate until someone brought it to light.

It's the myth that made Sidd Finch so enticing, that fuels so many "best shape" narratives and new pitch promises. We all, athletes and unathletic sportswriters, want to believe that there's genius trapped inside us, and that it's just a matter of puzzling out the combination to unlock it. That our art, our style is the next inefficiency, waiting for our own Billy Beane. It's why we root for underdogs, and why we're excited for the Mike Tauchmans and the Eurubiel Durazos, champions of skin-deep mediocrity.

Except we aren't anymore, really. The days of "Free X" have descended beyond the ring of irony and into obscurity. There are still Xs to be freed, or at least one X, duplicated endlessly: Mike Ford, Luke Voit, Max Muncy. The undervalued one-dimensional slugger demonstrated how the game hasn't quite culturally caught up to its logical extreme. But for those who don't fit the rather spacious mold, times are grimmer. As Rob Arthur revealed several months ago, there's been a marked increase in the number of sub-replacement relievers. It's the outcome of a greater number of teams forced to play out games without the talent to win them, but it's also emblematic of the modern tendency of teams to dispose of their disposable assets, burning through cost-controlled arms the way that man chopped down forests in *The Lorax*. Stuff just isn't built to outlive their original owners anymore.

It's unsurprising, given how well-mined the market for inefficiencies has been of late. The disciples of the early analytics departments, and the disciples of those, have proliferated the league, with only a few backwater holdouts. The league has grown smarter, but every team has learned the same lesson. In fact, the phenomenon creates a peculiar kind of feedback loop: As teams value a specific subset of players or skills, prospective athletes learn to increase their own marketability by conforming themselves to the demands of their prospective employers.

And that's tragic, in the way that the extinction of animals is tragic; a certain amount of biodiversity in baseball has been lost. Shortstops hit like outfielders. Pitchers don't hit at all. Only the catchers remain idiosyncratic, thanks to the defensive demands of their position; eventually they too will be required to produce like everyone else, or they'll meet the fate of their battery mates. A perfect economy requires perfect production.

I mentioned earlier that more and more, I leave thrift stores empty-handed. It is true that I am more discerning than in the past; my bookshelves are full, and there are more streaming films than I will ever be able to watch. But there are other factors at play.

Thrift stores are, in a way, the bond markets of retail. When the economy is rough and other retailers are struggling, more people look secondhand for their products. But as recently as last year, publications were noting a reversal of the trend: Companies like Goodwill and Savers were expanding despite a strong economy. Publications credited a heightened sense of environmentalism and a rejection of cutting-edge fashion as drivers behind the increase, though the more likely answer is the modern American economy hasn't showered its favors equally, particularly among the young.

But it is more than just the economy. Baseball and thrift stores share something else in common, evident in our current conversations about re-starting the sport: They live in the gray area between public service and private enterprise. Thrift stores provide affordable necessities to lower-class citizens, and collectibles and fashion for the middle-class. Because of the success of the latter, prices have gone up across the board. Especially in terms of clothing, the middle-class flight from fashion into vintage has instead carried the aftereffects of fashion, including its costs, into a territory where people just want clothes. But there's another factor in the rise of prices, in the form of the internet.

The Goodwills of the world have grown smarter, too, employing the internet to extract full value from their detritus. Ebay, similarly, has lost much of the charm it had as a new frontier around the turn of the century. Everything has a price point now; even individual taste is no match for the algorithm, because anything rare, no matter how niche its market, is a collectible to someone.

The internet has had the same effect on thrift stores that sabermetrics has had on baseball; its equivalent to OBP was the bar scanner. As detailed in Slate, the rise of second-party stores on eBay and Amazon birthed an entire industry of used-good salespeople, armed with PDAs and scanners, buying books for three dollars to sell online for five. The author, Michael Savitz, reports earning $60,000 by working nearly 80 hours a week; he makes it clear that this is not a vocation of his choosing. It's long hours, with no real creativity or individuality, skimming the cream off of a local establishment and flipping it to someone with a little more money on the other side of the country. And once the vocation exists, the obvious question arises: why wait to put the wares out on the shelves? Why allow value to exist at all?

Nothing is ruined. Thrift stores will continue to sell polo shirts and DVDs, and baseball will continue to exist and make or lose money, depending on who you believe. But as we continue to refine our knowledge, we lose something in the conquest for efficiency, a delight born out of the unknown. The problem isn't the efficiency itself; we can't blame the booksellers, or the people sweeping freeways to collect grams of platinum from damaged catalytic converters. The problem is a system that requires this sort of profit-skimming behavior in order to feed families (or, for corporations, maximize shareholder return).

Washington Nationals 2021

In times like these, with the 2020 season on the brink and the collective bargaining agreement close behind, it can often feel like the current situation is untenable. It can't keep going like this, even if we don't know what to do about it. But as with thrift stores, there's an equally irresistible feeling that it *has* to keep going, that it would be unimaginable to not have this broken, amazing sport. Both industries exist on an invisible foundation of friction, of chaos and unpredictability, even as both see their foundations buffed down to a perfect, untouchable polish. But if COVID-19 and its financial ramifications do, as some have suggested, make it such that the baseball that returns is fundamentally different than the baseball that came before, perhaps this is the time to lean in, and change the game even more. Fix bunting. Make defense more difficult. Create viable, alternate strategies. Add some chaos back into baseball. It's fun when no one knows quite where things are.

—Patrick Dubuque is an author of Baseball Prospectus.

Steve Dalkowski Dreaming

by Steven Goldman

We dream of being a pitcher, of starring in the major leagues. Depending on your age and your sense of historical perspective, you might imagine yourself as Walter Johnson, throwing harder than anyone else—hitting more batters than anyone else, too, but always feeling bad about it. You could picture yourself as a Tom Seaver or a David Cone, with all the stuff in the world but still being cerebral about it, thinking about so much more than burning 'em in there. There are so many models one could choose: You could be a Lefty Gomez, Jim Bouton, or Bill Lee, skilled, but not taking the whole thing too seriously, or a Lefty Grove, Bob Gibson, or Steve Carlton, powerful but treating each start like a mission to be survived instead of a game to be enjoyed.

Very few would dream of being Steve Dalkowski, the former Baltimore Orioles prospect who died of COVID-19 last week at the age of 80. Yet, there is something just as noble in Dalkowski's negative accomplishments—and accomplishments is what they are—as there is in the precision-engineered pitching of a Greg Maddux. You have to be very good to be that bad. Dalkowski had all of the stuff of the greatest pitchers but none of the command; his story is not one of failing to conquer his limitations, but striving against one of the cruelest hands that fate or genetics or personality can deal us: A desire to achieve great things which is almost but not quite matched by the ability to meet that goal.

As with Johnson, Grove, Bob Feller, and the rest of the hard-throwing pitchers who played before the advent of modern radar guns, we have to take the word of the players and coaches who saw Dalkowski pitch as to his velocity. He was a hard-drinking, maximum-effort pitcher who, if their memories are to be believed, consistently threw over 100 miles per hour. His was the Maltese Fastball, the stuff that dreams are made of. The problem is that velocity without command and control is still a good distance from utility. Dalkowski was the most effective towel you could design for a fish, the sleekest bathing suit intended to be worn by an astronaut, but that doesn't mean he wasn't beautiful: We can appreciate a journey even if it doesn't end at the intended destination.

Whether because of sloppy mechanics he couldn't calm, an inability to understand that a consistent 98 in the strike zone would likely be more effective than a consistent 110 out of it, or all that beer, Dalkowski could never make the adjustments that pitchers like Feller and Nolan Ryan made before him, possibly because he had so far to go: Feller, who never pitched in the minors, came up at 17 and spent three years walking almost seven batters per nine innings before settling in at 3.8 beginning when he was 20. Ryan started out walking over six batters per nine but gradually improved as his long career played out; for him to go from 6.2 walks per nine with the 1966 Greenville Mets to 3.7 with the 1989 Texas Rangers represents a 40 percent reduction. An equivalent improvement by Dalkowski would still have left him walking over 11 batters per nine innings.

Dalkowski was like *The Room* of pitchers, a player so bad he became good again. Cal Ripken, Sr., who both played with and managed Dalkowski, recalled in a 1979 *Sporting News* "where are they now" piece the occasion when the pitcher crossed up his catcher and his fastball, "hit the plate umpire smack in the mask. The mask broke all to pieces and the umpire wound up in the hospital for three days with a concussion. If they ever had a radar gun in those days, I'll bet Dalkowski would have been timed at 110 miles an hour."

Signed by the Orioles out of New Britain High in Connecticut in 1957, Dalkowski was sent to Kingsport in the Appalachian League, where he pitched 62 innings. He allowed only 22 hits in 62 innings, or 3.2 per nine, a number with no equivalent in major league history (though Aroldis Chapman came close in 2014), and also struck out 121 (17.6 per nine) and walked 129 (18.7). He was also charged with 39 wild pitches. That June, one of his fastballs clipped a Dodgers prospect named Bob Beavers and carried away part of his ear. "The first pitch was over the backstop, the second pitch was called a strike, I didn't think it was," Beavers said last year. "The third pitch hit me and knocked me out, so I don't remember much after that. I couldn't get in the sun for a while, and I never did play baseball again." Former minor leaguer Ron Shelton based the *Bull Durham* pitcher Nuke LaLoosh on Dalkowski. And yet, to see him as a figure of fun, an amusing loser, is to misunderstand something unique and strange.

Dalkowski kept on posting some of the strangest lines in baseball history. Pitching for the Stockton Ports of the Class C California League in 1960, he struck out 262 and walked 262 in 170 innings. Yet, he did improve, especially after pitching for Earl Weaver at Elmira in 1962. Weaver had previously had Dalkowski at Aberdeen in 1959, but wasn't ready to grapple with him then. This time he was. "I had grown more and more concerned about players with great physical abilities who could not learn to correct certain basic deficiencies no matter how much you instructed or drilled them," he related in his autobiography, *It's What You Learn After You Know It All That Counts*. He got permission from the Orioles to give all of his players the Stanford-Binet IQ test. "Dalkowski finished in the 1 percentile in his ability to understand facts. Steve, it was said to say, had the ability to do everything but learn." [sic]

IQ tests are problematic diagnostic tools, so take Weaver's estimate of Dalkowski's mental capabilities with a grain of salt. What's important is that even if he got to the right answer by way of the wrong reason, Weaver had learned something valuable. His insight was to stop asking Dalkowski to learn new pitches and just let him get by with the two that he had. Were Dalkowski a prospect today, that would have been a no-brainer: Can't develop a third pitch? The bullpen is right over there, sir. Player development wasn't like that then, but Weaver, temporarily Dalkowski's mentor, could let him work with what he had. According to Weaver, the pitcher responded: "In the final 57 innings he pitched that season Dalkowski gave up 1 earned run, struck out 110 batters, and walked only 11." It's not true—as per the *Elmira Star-Gazette*, as of late July, Dalkowski had walked 71 in 106 innings and finished with 114 in 160 innings, which means Dalkowski's control actually faded at the end of the season rather than improved—but that doesn't mean it didn't happen in some sense, just that it didn't happen that way. Again, it's the journey, not the destination, and his ERA was 3.04 so *something* had gone right.

Also along the way: The next spring, Orioles manager Billy Hitchcock was rooting for Dalkowski to make the team as a long-man—maybe Weaver had gotten through to him. There were things out of Weaver's control, like the universe's twisted sense of humor: that March, Dalkowski's elbow went "twang."

You sometimes read that it was the Orioles' insistence on Dalkowski learning the curve that did him in, but even if they hadn't learned their lesson, the injury was probably just a coincidence: Dalkowski had thrown an incredible number of pitches over the previous few years. Still, it testifies to the dangers of trying to get what you want and risking the loss of what you had. Dalkowski tried to come back, but the 110-mph stuff was gone. A pitcher with no control and no stuff is…a civilian. What followed were years of vagabond living, arrests for drunkenness. There were Alcoholics Anonymous meetings, assistance from baseball alumni associations, but none of it took. From the 1990s until the time of his passing he dwelt in an assisted living facility, suffering from alcohol-related dementia. He'd been a heavy drinker since his teenage years. As with all those pitches per game, there was a price to be paid. You make choices on the journey and some of them are irrevocable. It's like a fairy tale: "Bite of poison apple? Don't mind if I do."

In the aforementioned *Sporting News* profile, Chuck Stevens, the head of the Association of Professional Ballplayers of America, a ballplayer charity, said, "I've got nothing against drinking. I do it myself sometimes. But, I don't condone common drunkenness. We went through lots of heartache and many dollars, but Dalkowski didn't want to help himself and we weren't going to keep him drunk." The journey is *un*like a fairy tale: No one will come along and kiss it better, not if they're busy forming judgments.

In the end, we are left with a sort of philosophical chicken/egg conundrum: Is failing to meet your goals evidence of unfulfilled potential or the lack of it? Isn't what you did by definition what you were capable of doing? Or could you have broken through to something better with the right help, the right lucky break? These are unanswerable questions, and how we try to answer them may say more about us than about the people we're judging.

No pitcher ever has it easy. *All* pitchers must work hard. *All* pitchers must refine their craft. It's almost never just about *stuff*. Dalkowski dreaming is no insult to the great pitchers who made it; from Pete Alexander to Max Scherzer, they have all earned their way up. And yet, if it is true that we can only do as much as we can do, then the journey would be more of an adventure, the ultimate triumph or defeat more noble, if like Dalkowski we lacked 100 percent of the confidence, the command, the self-possession, the commitment, the resistance to making bad decisions that so many great players possess—to be gloriously human. Or, to put it more succinctly, it would be fun to be able to throw as hard as any person ever has. Even if just for a moment, and even if nothing more came of it than that, no one could say you hadn't lived life to the fullest.

—Steven Goldman is an author of Baseball Prospectus.

A Reward For A Functioning Society

by Cory Frontin and Craig Goldstein

On July 5, Nationals reliever Sean Doolittle said in the middle of a press conference regarding the restart of Major League Baseball and what would later be known as summer camp, "sports are like the reward of a functioning society." This sentence was amidst a much longer, thoughtful reply about the societal and health conditions under which MLB players were being brought back. It's a very similar sentiment to one Jane McManus used on April 7, when she discussed the White House's meeting with sports commissioners. She said "sports are the effect of a functioning society—not the precursor."

Both versions of the same sentiment spoke to a laudable ideal in the context of a country that was not addressing a rampaging virus, and opting instead to bring sports back for the feeling of normalcy rather than the reality of it. "Priorities," as McManus said.

On Wednesday, the NBA's Milwaukee Bucks conducted a wildcat/political strike, refusing to come out for Game 5 of their playoff series against the Orlando Magic. The Magic refused to accept the forfeit, and shortly thereafter other playoff series were threatened by player strikes. Eventually the league moved to postpone that day's games, folding to players leveraging their united power.

The backdrop against which these actions took place was the shooting by police of Jacob Blake. Blake was shot in the back seven times by police, as he attempted to get into his vehicle. He managed to survive the assault, but is paralyzed from the waist down.

⚾ ⚾ ⚾

The step taken to walk out, first by the Milwaukee Bucks, then subsequently by other NBA, WNBA, and MLB teams, was a step toward upholding the virtue of the sentiment described by McManus and Doolittle. But that sentiment does not align with the broad history of sports in this and other countries, a history that contradicts the core of the idealistic statement.

Sports have been a significant part of American society for most of its existence, expanding in importance and influence in recent years. The idea that society was functioning in a way that was worthy of the reward of sports for most of that time is laughable. Much of America is not functioning and has not functioned for Black people, full stop. The oppressed people at the center of this political act by players, specifically Black players, in concert throughout the NBA and in fits and starts throughout Major League Baseball, have not known a society that functions for them rather than *because* of them.

Politics has been part of the sports landscape since the inception of sport, but for just about as long people have bemoaned its presence. Sports are to be an escape, it is said. An escape from what, though? A functioning society?

No, the presence of sports has never signified a cultural or political system that is on the up and up. Rather, the presence of sports *reflect and reinforce the society that produces them.*

⚾   ⚾   ⚾

The Negro Leagues were born out of societal dysfunction. The need for entirely separate leagues, composed of Black and Latino players barred from the Major Leagues because of racism? That is not a functioning society, and yet there were sports.

Even the integration of players from the Negro Leagues resulted in a transfer of power and wealth from Black-owned businesses and communities and into white ones, mirroring the dysfunction that had bled into every aspect of American society at the time. Japheth Knopp noted in the Spring 2016 Baseball Research Journal:

> *The manner in which integration in baseball—and in American businesses generally—occurred was not the only model which was possible. It was likely not even the best approach available, but rather served the needs of those in already privileged positions who were able to control not only the manner in which desegregation occurred, but the public perception of it as well in order to exploit the situation for financial gain. Indeed, the very word integration may not be the most applicable in this context because what actually transpired was not so much the fair and equitable combination of two subcultures into one equal and more homogenous group, but rather the reluctant allowance—under certain preconditions—for African Americans to be assimilated into white society.*

To understand the value of a movement, though, is not to understand how it is co-opted by ownership, but to know the people it brings together and what they demand. When Jackie Robinson—the player who demarcated the inevitability of the end of the Negro leagues—attended the March on Washington for Jobs and Freedom in 1963, he did so with his family and marched alongside the people. He stood alongside hundreds of thousands to fight for their common civil and labor rights. "The moral arc of the universe is long," many freedom fighters have echoed, "but it bends towards justice." The bend, it is less frequently said, happens when a great mass of people place the moral arc of the universe on their knee and apply force, as Jackie, his family, and thousands of others did that day.

⚾ ⚾ ⚾

Of course, taking the moral arc of the universe down from the mantle and bending it is not without risk. Perhaps the outsized influence of athletes is itself a mark of a dysfunctional society, but, nonetheless, hundreds of athletes woke up on Wednesday morning with the power to bring in millions of dollars in revenues. That very power, as we would come to find out, was matched with the equal and opposite power to *not* bring those revenues. That power, in hands ranging from the Milwaukee Bucks, to Kenny Smith in the *Inside the NBA* Studio, from the unexpected ally, Josh Hader, and his largely white teammates to the notably Black Seattle Mariners, would be exercised for a single demand: the end to state violence against Black people. Not unlike the March itself, it sat at the intersection of the civil rights of Black Americans and bold labor action. The March on Washington stood in the face of a false notion of integration—against an integration of extraction but not one of equality—and proposed something different. Just the same, the acts of solidarity of August 26, 2020 will be remembered in stark defiance of MLB's BLM-branded, but ultimately empty displays on opening weekend.

Bold defiance like this can never be without risk. By choosing to exercise this power, the Milwaukee Bucks took a risk. They risked vitriol and backlash from those they disagreed with. They risked fines or seeing their contracts voided, as a walkout like this is prohibited by their CBA. They risked forfeiting a playoff game, one that, as the No. 1 seed in the playoffs, they'd worked all year to attain. They didn't know how Orlando would respond. It wasn't clear that other teams throughout the league would follow suit in solidarity. And it wasn't known the league would accept these actions and moderately co-opt them by "postponing" games that would have featured no players.

If the league reschedules the games, some of the athletes' risk—their shared sacrifice—will be diminished, in retrospect. But they did not know any of that when they took that risk. And it is often left to athletes to take these risks when others in society won't, especially those of their same socioeconomic status and levels of influence.

It is athletes, specifically BIPOC athletes, that take them, though, because they live with the risk of being something other than white in this country every day. They are no strangers to the realities of police brutality. It seems incongruous then, to say that sports are a reward for a functioning society when we rely on athletes to lead us closer to being a functioning society. Luckily, our beloved athletes, WNBA players first and foremost among them, understand what sports truly are: a pipebender for the moral arc of the universe.

> *—Craig Goldstein is editor in chief of Baseball Prospectus. Cory Frontin is an author of Baseball Prospectus.*

Index of Names

Antuna, Yasel 74, 90
Armenteros, Rogelio 79
Avila, Alex 75
Bacus, Dakota 42
Barrett, Aaron 79
Bell, Josh 16
Bonifácio, Emilio 75
Braymer, Ben 44
Cabrera, Asdrúbal 18
Castro, Starlin 20
Cate, Tim 89
Cavalli, Cade 80, 87
Cluff, Jackson 93
Corbin, Patrick 46
Cronin, Matt 91
De La Rosa, Jeremy 93
Denaburg, Mason 92
Fedde, Erick 48
Finnegan, Kyle 50
García, Luis 22
Gomes, Yan 24
Guerra, Javy 52
Hand, Brad 81
Harper, Ryne 54
Harris, Will 56
Harrison, Josh 26
Henry, Cole 82, 90
Hudson, Daniel 58
Infante, Sammy 92
Kendrick, Howie 28
Kieboom, Carter 30
Lara, Andry 91
Lester, Jon 60
McGowin, Kyle 62
Mendoza, Drew 88
Quintana, Roismar 93
Rainey, Tanner 64
Robles, Victor 32
Romero, Seth 82
Ross, Joe 83
Rutledge, Jackson 84, 88
Sanchez, Adrían 76
Sánchez, Aníbal 66
Scherzer, Max 68
Schwarber, Kyle 34
Soto, Juan 36
Stevenson, Andrew 77
Strasburg, Stephen 85
Suero, Wander 70
Thames, Eric 38
Turner, Trea 40
Voth, Austin 72
Williams, Austen 86
Zimmerman, Ryan 78

For the Joy of Keeping Score

THIRTY81 Project is an ongoing graphic design project focused on the ballparks of baseball. Since being established in 2013, scorecards have been a fundemantal part of the effort. Each two-page card is uniquely ballpark-centric — there are 30 variants — and designed with both beginning and veteran scorekeepers in mind. Evolving over the years with suggestions from fans, broadcasters, and official scorers, the sheets are freely available to everyone as printable letter-size PDFs at the project webshop: www.THIRTY81Project.com

Download, Print, Score, Repeat …

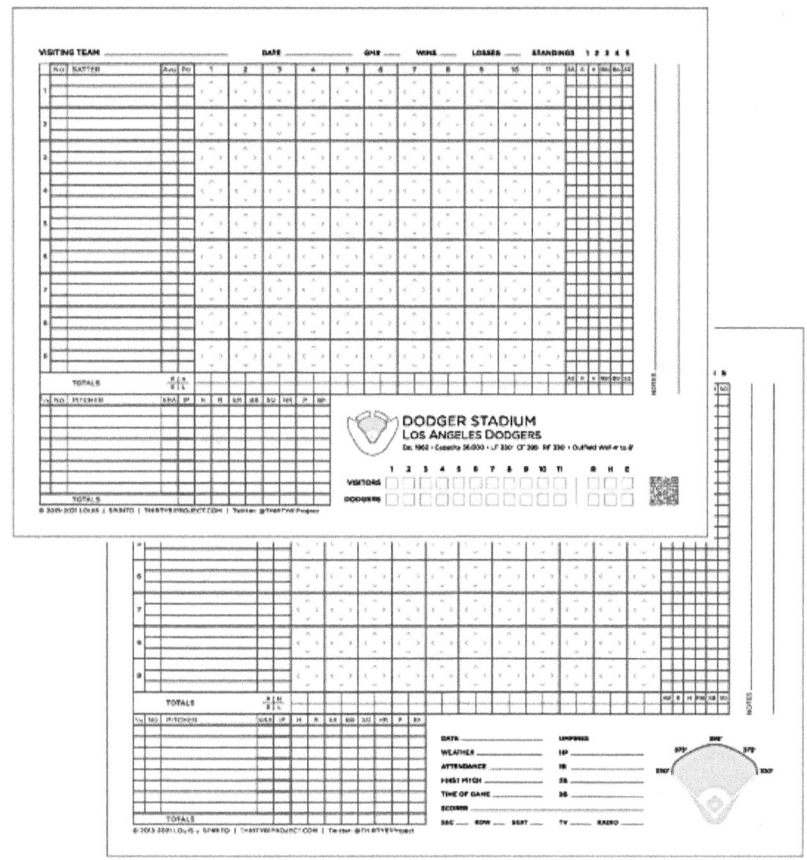

Scorecard design ©2013-2021 Louis J. Spirito | THIRTY81Project